CONTEMPORARY BRITAIN

Second Edition

Ruth Blakey M.A.
Teacher of Modern Studies
Boclair Academy, Dunbarton Division, Strathclyde

Wilson Blakey M.A. (Hons.) Dip.Ed.
Assistant Rector, Vale of Leven Academy,
Dunbarton Division, Strathclyde

Bob McKay B.A. (Hons.)
Assistant Head Teacher, St Augustine's
Secondary School, Glasgow Division, Strathclyde

Oliver & Boyd

Contents

Introduction

The study of contemporary Britain – our country in the present day – is complicated. A glance at the contents page will show the wide variety of topics to be covered.

The authors have arranged material in three parts and in each part they try to show how the individual is involved in the working of contemporary Britain.

Part 1 Politics

Politics is the study of why and how societies reach decisions. Societies can be small groups of people, members of a club, a gang, neighbours or large groups such as a local community or a whole nation. Nearly everyone in Britain over the age of eighteen is entitled to vote and if they do not choose to vote or do so without careful thought, then they can hardly criticise those who have been chosen by those who did vote.

Part 2 The Economy

Economics is the study of how and why societies make use of things they make or acquire. Britain is a major trading and manufacturing nation and it is important to know how goods are made and used because we are all producers and consumers in some way.

Part 3 Society

Society is made up of different individuals and groups. We are all members of different groups: family, school, factory workforce, village, town, city, region, nation. Wherever people are gathered together there may be disagreements, arguments, and disputes. A way has to be found to settle these conflicts and to reach agreement on some form of co-operation. It is hard to escape being involved in society.

In this way the authors illustrate the fact that people do not live in isolation from each other and the rest of the world. Our actions and decisions affect other people, who in turn want to help us to be healthy, teach us things, make things for us, sell us things, stop us hurting ourselves or others, and give advice or assistance when it is needed.

No book is large enough to include a complete picture of life in Britain today. However, the authors have collected a wide variety of material for the reader to study: straight text giving information and explanation; photographs; diagrams to help with the understanding of ideas and relationships; graphs and tables giving facts and statistics; and simulation case studies (short stories or descriptions of imaginary people in real situations).

To this information the reader and/or teacher should add other resources which are similar or different to those in the book. Finally the whole mass of information should be compared with and added to the reader's own experience. This is a source book. Choose the bits you find valuable and use the questions included as a check on whether you do have an understanding of contemporary Britain.

Introduction to the Second Edition

The second edition of *Contemporary Britain* takes account of the sweeping changes in politics, economy and society of Britain in the 1980s. In addition to updated statistical material, photographs and text, there are important new sections which reflect issues of growing concern in Britain today.

Part 1 incorporates the many subtle changes in the British political system, including the development of new political parties and pressures for changes in representation.

Part 2 reflects the major and dramatic changes in the British economy in recent years: the level and type of state involvement; problems facing major industries; national economic problems and solutions, industrial relations legislation.

Part 3 has been expanded considerably. In particular, increased coverage has been given to the Welfare State, and issues relating to law and order, the changing role of women, Britain as a multi-cultural society, increased leisure and the impact of technology.

PART 1

Politics

1. British Government

Britain is widely regarded as having a democratic system of government. That is to say, the British people have a say in how the country should be run. You will be able to decide in the next few pages to what extent this statement is true. No country allows its people to take all the decisions all the time, sometimes because it is not physically possible to ask their opinion, and sometimes because the country is run by a dictator or by an elite group who are not interested in the opinions of the people. The British system falls somewhere between.

A system of governing a country which claims to be democratic allows for disagreements and argument, usually on the understanding that, once a decision has been taken, the minority will allow the majority to rule, in return for some concessions. There is often conflict as to how to choose a government and what the government should be allowed to do once chosen. The study of British government can be difficult, partly because many of its rules are unwritten **conventions** and partly because it is complicated. By following the fortunes of two imaginary politicians, its study can be made less difficult.

General Election Special

Introducer: Today, Thursday, 29 October, is **election** day throughout the United Kingdom. The **polls** closed just a short time ago. This marks the climax of a three-week campaign. We are now going over to our political reporter, James Neil, to see how the campaign and results have gone in Newtown, Scotland.

Neil: Good evening, and welcome to the packed Newtown Town Hall where the count is taking place. While we are waiting for the result let me explain what the election has meant to the people of Newtown. There are two constituencies, one a safe Labour seat, and the other a marginal seat held narrowly by the Conservatives at the last election. Since early this morning, workers of all parties have been making sure their promised voters have gone to the poll.

It looks as if it will be a very close contest in Newtown South constituency. No party is sure of victory. In the last five elections the majority has never been greater than 2000. The Conservative **candidate**, James Falconer, is a local estate

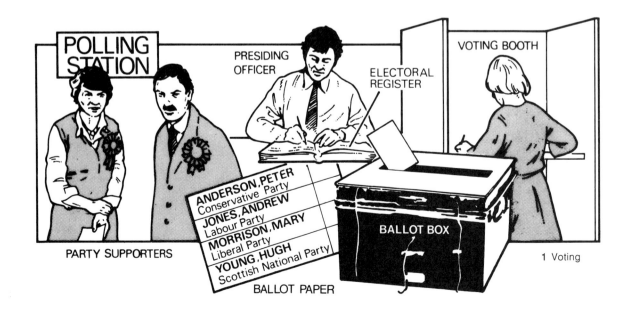

POLLING STATION

PRESIDING OFFICER

ELECTORAL REGISTER

VOTING BOOTH

ANDERSON,PETER
Conservative Party
JONES,ANDREW
Labour Party
MORRISON,MARY
Liberal Party
YOUNG,HUGH
Scottish National Party

BALLOT BOX

PARTY SUPPORTERS

BALLOT PAPER

1 Voting

agent who has campaigned mainly on price rises and local issues. Hugh Daly is a trade union offical sponsored by his union as Labour candidate. The other two candidates are Michael Rodgers, Liberal, and Sue Thomson, Scottish National Party. There are suggestions that the vote will be so close that a recount may be required.

In Newtown North the sitting MP, Peter Brown, is again contesting the seat for Labour. He has been a Member of Parliament here since his win in a by-election sixteen years ago. He is also a member of the Cabinet. His main opponent, Sarah Wharton, Conservative, has led a vigorous campaign, but it would require a massive swing to unseat Mr Brown from his very safe Labour constituency. Of the other three opponents, Stuart Armstrong, SNP, Vicky Dawson, SDP, and Peter Webster, Independent, the predictions are that only the SNP candidate has a chance of saving his **deposit**.

Both constituencies have had a very heavy poll: nearly 80%.

It will be some time before the results are announced. So I have an opportunity to talk to

2 Campaigning

Who can vote?

All British citizens over the age of 18, except . . .

 Members of the immediate Royal Family

 Peers in the House of Lords

 Convicted criminals and inmates of mental institutions

3 Who can vote?

two of the main contestants in Newtown, Mr Brown and Mr Falconer. Mr Brown, the national opinion polls suggest that you may well be returning with your party to government. Are you hoping to be back in the Cabinet?

Brown: Well, the Prime Minister decides on the Cabinet, but I would agree that the Labour Party will have an overall majority in the House of Commons.

Falconer: I would not accept that. My own canvas returns in Newtown South constituency clearly point to a Conservative victory and I believe that the Conservative Party nationally will not only hold safe seats but will win marginals such as my own.

Neil: As a first-time candidate, Mr Falconer, might I ask you how you see your role as an MP?

Falconer: If elected, I would look forward to representing all the people of Newtown South constituency and participating as a backbench MP in a Conservative government.

Neil: Mr Brown, as a man who has successfully fought many campaigns, what changes have you noticed in campaigns over the years?

Brown: Some things like canvassing, leafleting, public meetings and hard work never change, but in recent years television, radio and public opinion polls have played an increasing part.

Neil: Thank you both very much, I believe you now have to return to the Town Hall as the Returning Officer is about to announce the results in both constituencies.

Returning Officer: I James Morris, being the Returning Officer for the constituencies of Newtown North and South, declare that the total number of votes cast for each candidate in Newtown North was as follows:

Armstrong, Stuart	11 923
Brown, Peter	23 506
Dawson, Victoria	3 704
Webster, Peter	208
Wharton, Sarah	12 047

I therefore declare that the said Peter Brown has

4 Tony Benn making his acceptance speech after a returning officer has read election results

been elected to serve as member of Parliament for the Newtown North constituency.

The total number of votes cast for each candidate in the Newtown South constituency was as follows:

Daly, Hugh	15 417
Falconer, James	15 742
Rodgers, Michael	4 029
Thomson, Susan	9 418
Spoiled papers	27

and I declare that . . .

Neil: Before returning you to the studio let me sum up. Labour have held their safe seat. The Conservatives have held their marginal with a reduced majority. The SNP on their first attempt have come third in both constituencies. The Liberal and SDP candidates and the independent have lost their deposits since none received a large enough share of the total **vote** of their constituency. And now back to the studio for the national results.

ELECTION RESULTS

Reporter: With only a few results to come, none of which are likely to change hands, we can predict with some certainty that the final result will be:

Labour	328 MPs
Conservative	292 MPs
Others	30 MPs

A very small swing to the Labour Party means that the Queen will be inviting the leader of the Labour Party to form a government. The overall majority is six.

We have in the studio representatives of the Labour, Conservative, Alliance and SNP parties.

Ladies and gentlemen, can I ask you for your first reactions?

Labour spokesperson: Well, we are delighted to have won and, although the overall majority is only six, the opposition is not united and we do have a majority of thirty-six over our nearest rivals.

Conservative spokesperson: I think another election within eighteen months is very likely since the new government's majority is so small.

Liberal/SDP Alliance spokesperson: This election again demonstrates the basic unfairness of the British electoral system. The Labour and Conservative Parties each have 39% of the total vote cast, yet Labour have more than 50% of the seats, and Conservatives have well over 40% of the seats. The Liberals, SDP and other smaller parties have fewer seats than the national vote entitles them to.

SNP spokesperson: I must agree with the last speaker. The two major parties support the present voting system only because they benefit from its unfairness.

Labour spokesperson: That is hardly true. We support the present system because it is easy to operate, understood by the **electorate** and it is democratic. Furthermore, it provides for stability and continuity of government and avoids the type of coalitions to be found in other Western European states.

Reporter: Perhaps we can look at alternative voting systems and examine their possible effects on parties and government in the UK.

Questions

1. Describe how you would go about voting, from entering the polling station to leaving it.
2. If you were a candidate, what would you do to try to win an election?
3. Why are some people not allowed to vote?
4. Describe, with as much detail as you can, the winning candidates in the two Newtown constituencies.

Voting Systems

The present system is the 'simple majority' or 'first past the post' system. The voter puts a cross on the ballot paper beside the name of the candidate of his/her choice and the candidate receiving more votes than any other single candidate in each constituency wins. If you look at the two results in Newtown, you will note that neither winner received 50% or more of the total vote cast.

Nationally, the party that wins in more constituencies (i.e. has more seats in Parliament) than any other forms a government, although they may not have received the majority of votes over the country. This system tends to favour the two major parties.

The supporters of a change in the voting system, for example, the Liberal Party, point to the statistics such as the following from the 1974 (February) election to support their case.

(a) The Labour Party won five more seats than the Conservative Party (and formed a government), but they had 1% fewer votes than the Conservatives.

(b) The total votes cast for each party divided by the number of seats gained, show that the Liberals had approximately one seat per 40 000 voters, whereas Labour and Conservative had one seat per 40 000–60 000 voters.

PROPORTIONAL REPRESENTATION

Proportional representation is any electoral system which would try to distribute the seats in the House of Commons between the parties in a way which ensured that the percentage of seats for each party more closely reflected the percentage of votes cast for each party. The following table demonstrates the change in seat distribution which would have taken place in February 1974 under one of the sytems of proportional representation.

	Labour	Conservative	Liberal	Others
Actual seats	301	296	14	24
Prop.rep. seats	236	241	123	35

The following are two methods of proportional representation.

Alternative Vote

In this system, if there are more than two candidates, the voter numbers them in his/her order of preference (1 for first choice, 2 for second choice). The first choices are then counted. If one candidate

5 Election results since 1966 (*NB* In 1983 the number of seats was increased from 635 to 650 by the Boundaries Commission)

Year	Labour		Conservative		Liberal		Others	
	Seats	Votes (%)	Seats	Votes (%)	Seats	Votes (%)	Seats	Votes (%)
1966	363	48	253	42	12	9	2	1
1970	287	43	330	46	6	7	7 (SNP 3)	3
Feb '74	301	38	296	39	14	19	24 (SNP 7)	4
Oct '74	319	39	276	36	13	18	27 (SNP 11)	7
1979	268	37	339	44	11	14	17 (SNP 2)	4
1983	209	28	397	42	23*	25*	21 (SNP 2)	5

* including SDP

is the first choice of 51% of all voters, he/she is declared the winner. If no-one has achieved this, the candidate coming last is eliminated and the second choices of the voters who supported him/her are distributed among the other candidates. This process continues until one candidate has 51% of the votes.

The National List System

This requires each political party to provide a list of up to 650 candidates in order of preference. The electorate vote for the party of their choice rather than an individual candidate. On the basis of the total number of votes cast for each party nationally, the appropriate percentage of seats in the House of Commons would be given to each party. For example, if the Liberal/SDP Alliance Parties received 20% of the national vote they would be given 20% of the seats in the House of Commons. This would be about 120 seats and therefore the first 120 candidates on the Alliance list would become Members of Parliament.

Questions

1. What are the advantages of the 'first past the post' voting system?
2. Why do the Liberal Party and the SDP favour a change in the electoral system?
3. Draw a pie chart to show the percentage of votes for each party in 1983.
4. Draw a bar graph to show the seats won by each party in both elections in 1974.
5. Which voting system do you think is fairest? Give reasons for your answer.
6. Describe what is happening in photograph 4 and what will happen immediately afterwards.

The Parties

In the text on the General Election several political parties were mentioned. We should therefore examine the parties, their principles and beliefs. The two major parties are the Conservative and Labour parties, although in recent years they have lost some of their support to the minor parties: the Liberals, SDP, the Scottish and Welsh Nationalists and several other parties in Northern Ireland. Each party offers alternative proposals for Britain's **economic, political, social** and international development. The parties do not disagree on every issue: for example, in foreign affairs the Labour and Conservative parties are often in agreement. The major areas of disagreement are in social and economic matters. It should also be noted that each party is not itself totally united on every issue, and is made up of people with quite a wide range of ideas and beliefs.

THE LABOUR PARTY

The Labour Party has its origins in various working-class and intellectual movements of the late nineteenth and early twentieth centuries. The different groups within the party share the common goal of the redistribution of wealth by the taxation of the well-off, by government action. They do not always agree on the extent or type of action, however. The left wing of the party (e.g. the Tribune Group) are in favour of the public ownership of wealth on behalf of the working classes. The centre and right of the party (e.g. the Manifesto Group) prefer to pursue the redistribution of wealth by the taxation of private wealth.

The Labour Party in the 1920s became the alternative to the Conservatives and, in 1923 and 1929, formed short-lived minority governments. In 1945 they formed their first majority government and also won the 1950 election by a narrow majority. During this period they introduced considerable **nationalisation** and established the National Health Service. They were also in power between 1964 and 1970 and from 1974 to 1979.

Labour believe that government must play a major role in the economy, not only by public ownership, but also by control and regulation. They are more concerned with the ideas of the **community,** its needs and demands, than with individual enterprise. Their ideal is a redistribution of wealth either by taxation or increased public ownership.

Some examples of the ideals of the Labour Party are:
● *Education.* They believe in **comprehensive** education for all and an abandonment of selective schools together with an unwillingness to support private schools.
● *Housing.* They tend to support an expansion of the public sector, i.e the building of local **authority** housing for rent. They have also been responsible for legislation to control private landlords.
● *Nationalisation.* They believe that some firms and industries should be bought by the government and run by them. For example, in 1977 the shipbuilding industry was taken into the public sector.

THE CONSERVATIVE PARTY

The Conservative Party is the oldest major British

political party. Today, like the Labour Party, it reflects a mixture of different philosophies with a common goal. It includes those who support completely free enterprise (business with little or no government interference) and others who accept some government responsibility but would not support the 'socialism' of the Labour Party.

Before 1945, the Conservative Party held power more often than any other party. Since 1945, their periods in power have been 1951 to 1964 and 1970 to 1974 and from 1979. The Conservative philosophy hinges on the support of the individual, free and private enterprise and a limited government role in the economy. In recent years this has expressed itself in their idea of 'choice'.

● *Education.* Although giving some support to comprehensive education, they have fought to retain selective schools and have argued for 'choice' within the comprehensive system.

● *Housing.* They are less inclined to support local authority housing and **subsidised** rents and favour large-scale council house sales and private house building.

● *Privatisation.* Although they will continue to operate some of the nationalised industries, they prefer to sell others back to the private sector.

THE LIBERAL PARTY

The parliamentary power of the Liberal Party has declined throughout this century. When the Labour Party became the accepted alternative party to the Conservatives, the Liberals began to lose ground and, since 1945, they have always had fewer than twenty MPs. The Liberal Party see themselves as a radical alternative to the two main parties. They oppose the ideas of public ownership but prefer profit-sharing schemes to complete private enter-

pise. They are strong supporters of individual and human rights, social reform, federalism and a complete reform of the tax system. Internationally, they were strongly in favour of UK membership of the European Community (EEC) and they support NATO.

In 1977, the party had some experience of power when they entered the Lib–Lab Pact. This was a short-term measure to prevent the Labour Government from losing a 'no confidence' vote to the Conservatives and having to call a General Election. The Liberal Party, under David Steel, agreed to support the Labour Party in return for consultation over legislative proposals. Though it gave the party a taste of power, it did not increase its popularity.

THE SOCIAL DEMOCRATIC PARTY

The SDP grew rapidly in the 1980s and for a time caught the imagination of the voters and the media. Its origins lay in the growing disenchantment which some right-wing Labour supporters felt with changes which had been taking place within the Labour Party. **Constitutional** changes, shifts in policy and action had made some members feel increasingly isolated.

In early 1981, four of these politicians joined together to announce the beginning of the SDP. They were nicknamed the 'Gang of Four', and stated 'We have broken the mould of British politics. The people of Britain now have a real alternative to the extremism of Left and Right.' Support for the party quickly increased. Opinion polls showed this new party to be a real threat to the two-party system; a total of 25 Labour and 1 Conservative MPs defected to the SDP. In several by-elections the popularity of the SDP was tested and there were some victories and some near misses.

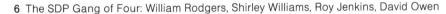

6 The SDP Gang of Four: William Rodgers, Shirley Williams, Roy Jenkins, David Owen

Agreement was reached with the Liberal Party that, rather than have both parties fighting for the middle ground in politics, they would form an didates in the 650 constituencies were agreed to on a 50:50 basis, and it was hoped that the Alliance 50:50 basis, and it was hoped that the Alliance would at least hold the balance of power after the 1983 election, if not outright victory. In the event, although the Liberal/SDP Alliance won the support of almost 8 million voters, they only got 23 MPs, because of the system of voting in Britain. The Alliance had won 25% of the votes but only 3.5% of the seats.

During the 1980s, the SDP have gradually developed policies, by consulting their members in 'rolling' conferences. They believe in the mixed economy; some form of incomes policy; and an increase in democracy in industry. They are for continued membership of the European Community and are strongly in favour of multilateral disarmament. However, their main policy has to be for proportional representation, to have the same support in the House of Commons as they potentially have in the country. If proportional representation does not come, many SDP members may become disillusioned with holding the middle ground of British politics.

OTHER PARTIES

Scottish and Welsh **Nationalists** are in favour of Scotland and Wales being separate States. They believe that they are separate nations historically, economically and culturally, and that their interests are not best served by a UK Parliament. On the major social and economic issues they tend to be internally divided, since they have within their membership people of socialist, conservative and liberal views.

From the late 1960s until the General Election of 1979, the Nationalists enjoyed a considerable electoral revival. However, in recent years their support has declined, perhaps revealing the extent to which many of their supporters were registering a protest vote against the two major parties rather than genuinely believing in independence. The rise of the Liberal/SDP Alliance has certainly affected their popularity.

In Northern Ireland, the major parties have retained some separate identity from the mainland

7   Summary of major party viewpoints

	Conservative	Labour
● Basic philosophy	People are able to get on without government aid. Free enterprise and choice.	Government must be involved to create a fairer and more compassionate society.
● Economy	Encourage private enterprise and cut government spending.	Plan for industrial development. Nationalise industries.
Taxation	Few taxes, as low as possible to allow people to spend their own money.	Range of taxes to take money from those who can afford it to help the less well-off.
● Wages and prices	Give top workers high wages to reward effort, encourage others to work harder and stop 'brain drain'.	Reduce gap between well-off and less well-off. Tie increases to prductivity. Limit all income, and control prices.
● Social services	Increase chances to pay for services in education, private medicine, sale of council houses. Increase incentive to work.	Free health and social services. Widen range of services to all in need.
● Education	Keep selective schools. Keep fee-paying schools.	Encourage comprehensive system. Put fee-paying schools outside state system.
● Foreign policy	Resist threat of Communism. Get better deal in EEC. Maintain strong links with USA.	Establish better relations with superpowers. Review membership of EEC.
● Government	Keep hereditary peers in House of Lords.	Decrease powers of House of Lords.
● Home affairs	Keen on 'law and order'. Severely limit immigration.	Limit immigration. Keen on good community relations.
● Defence	Maintain position of strength through independent nuclear deterrent and links with USA. Negotiate disarmament cautiously.	Review need for independent nuclear deterrent. Encourage world-wide disarmament, perhaps giving a lead.
● Industry	Encourage investment and initiative to regenerate industry and so reduce unemployment.	Increase public spending to move country out of slump and provide jobs.

parties. The right-wing parties include the Ulster Unionists and the Democratic Unionists, while the main left-wing party is the SDLP. It is a feature of Irish politics that many people vote along religious lines, with Protestants voting for Unionist candidates and Catholics supporting the SDLP or Sinn Fein.

The voter may also choose to vote for one of the fringe parties (if these parties put up a candidate), such as the Communist Party, the Socialist Workers Party or the National Front. There are also several other small parties called single issue parties. One example is the Ecology Party whose members campaign for an improvement in the environment.

The tradition of the 'independent' candidate has largely disappeared except at by-elections. Most of these candidates tend to stand as a joke, or for the publicity, rather than for any hope of coming close to winning.

One other choice for the electorate, and one exercised by more than 20% of the electorate at most General Elections, is to abstain and not vote at all.

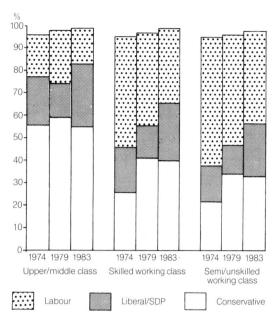

9 How Britain voted by social class

Questions

1. What are the main aims of each of the four biggest parties?
2. What are the policies of the two major parties on (a) unemployment, (b) housing, (c) defence, (d) capital punishment?
3. Look at Fig. **8**. Which parties would be described as extremists, and which as moderates?
4. What are the views of the Liberal Party, the SDP and the SNP on major issues?

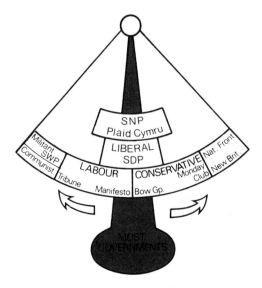

8 The political pendulum

Parliament

THE HOUSE OF COMMONS

Peter Brown and James Falconer have been elected to serve as members of the House of Commons. This is the elected House of **Parliament** with 650 members.

Peter Brown, being a member of the party having a majority in the House of Commons, will sit on the benches to the right of the Speaker. (The Speaker is the MP who chairs the House of Commons, elected by fellow members and responsible for the conduct of business and **debate**. It is the Speaker who applies the rules, procedures and traditions of the House. The Speaker only votes when the 'ayes' and 'noes' tie.) Since Mr Brown has been selected by the Prime Minister to be Secretary of State for Scotland, he will occupy a front bench seat. Behind him there are junior **ministers** and then backbench MPs. On the Speaker's left, the Conservative Party, being the next largest party in the House after this election, occupy the benches of Her Majesty's Opposition. The Shadow Cabinet headed by the Leader of the Opposition occupy the front benches. The task of all Opposition MPs is to examine and criticise the activities of government while presenting alternative proposals themselves.

The maximum life of a Parliament is five years because convention requires that a General Election must be called at least every five years. The

1 Prime Minister
2 Leader of the Opposition
3 Government Front Bench
4 Opposition Front Bench
5 Back Benches
6 Other Opposition Parties
7 Speaker
8 Mace
9 Dispatch Box
10 Hansard and Press gallery
11 Special galleries for peers,
    distinguished strangers, etc.

10 The House of Commons

11 The State Opening of Parliament in the House of Lords

Prime Minister, however, may request the Queen to call an election at any time within the five years. If the government is defeated on a vote of confidence in the House of Commons, convention requires that the government resign in order that another government, commanding a majority in the House, may take over, or, as is more likely, that a General Election be held.

The monarch is responsible for the State Opening of Parliament and for reading the Queen's Speech. In this speech, the government's proposals and intentions for the coming parliamentary session are announced. They are, in fact, drawn up by the Cabinet, and presented to the monarch. After the Speech, Parliament debates and votes on its content; the first test of the government's majority in the House of Commons

The following general points about debates in the House should be noted:

● Members take turns to speak when called on by the Speaker after 'catching his eye'.
● Parliamentary privilege: all MPs enjoy complete freedom of speech within Parliament. This protects their interests and encourages the fullest debate possible.
● Unparliamentary language: there is an accepted code that no member of the House will use any form of offensive language to other members. The Speaker applies this rule and anyone refusing to

retract such language may be 'named' and removed from the House.

● 'Hansard' is the official report of every word that is said in both the House of Lords and the House of Commons.

● 'Maiden' speech is the first speech in the House by a new member.

● The **quorum** for the House of Commons is forty and for the House of Lords is three.

● The guillotine is a device used by the government to limit discussion and debate. It sets a timetable for each stage of a bill, at the end of which a vote must be taken.

MAKING A LAW

The main task of Parliament is legislation, i.e. the process of law making. For this process there is an established procedure.

1 *White paper.* Most proposed legislation appears as a White Paper, thus giving the government time to take into account comments and criticisms from the public and pressure groups.

2 *The First Reading.* All proposed legislation begins as a printed document known as a Bill. The Minister or Private Member responsible for the Bill stands and says, 'Mr Speaker, Sir, a Bill'. This is the formal announcement and presentation of the Bill to the House. MPs then go away and read the Bill.

3 *The Second Reading.* This allows the House to debate fully the principles and intentions of the Bill. At the end of the debate a vote may be called. At this point the members of Parliament file into the division lobbies to vote yes or no to the principles of the Bill. If the majority vote is against it, the Bill falls. If the majority supports it, the process continues to the next stage.

4 *The Committee Stage.* At this point the Bill is examined in great detail and amendments are offered, debated, accepted or rejected. The Committee will normally be a standing committee of the House of Commons. Its make-up in terms of political parties will be a reflection of party strengths in the full House. Some Bills (e.g. finance Bills and constitutional Bills) are examined by a Committee of the Whole House of Commons (all MPs are members of this committee).

5 *The Report Stage.* This allows the House to be informed of the work and findings of the Committee and for any amendments to be moved and voted on by all MPs.

6 *The Third Reading.* This is the final debate and vote by the House.

If the Bill is not financial it goes to the House of Lords and through the same process. If it passes through the Lords it will go back to the Commons and then to the Queen for signature (Royal Assent). It will then become an Act of Parliament.

THE HOUSE OF LORDS

The House of Lords is the other house in Parliament. It has over 1000 members, none of whom are elected. Its members include hereditary peers, life peers, law lords, archbishops (of York and Canterbury) and 24 bishops of the Church of England.

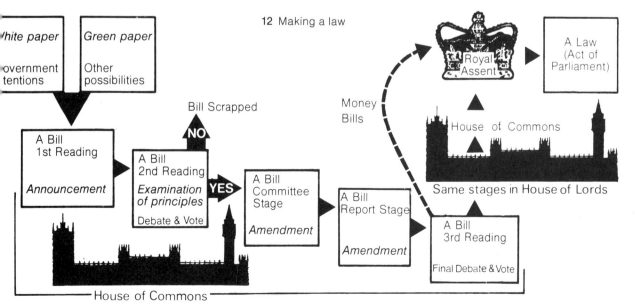

12 Making a law

Although the importance of the Lords has decreased in the twentieth century, it still has two important functions. It debates Bills (except Money Bills), especially those parts which may have been hurried through the House of Commons. Occasionally it introduces Bills. The Lords can vote against a Bill but cannot delay its passage for more than a year.

The House of Lords has been criticised for being non-elected, for having a Conservative bias, for having too many hereditary peers, and for its poor attendance figures. It does, however, allow, by the Life Peerages Act of 1958, the appointment of citizens who have made an important contribution to society. Also, by the 1963 Peerages Act, hereditary peers can give up their titles.

Clearly, the House of Lords is out of date in its present form, but the best method to reform it is not so clear.

THE MONARCHY

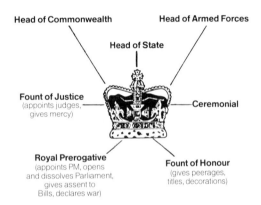

13 The role of the monarch

The monarch has many constitutional powers, as shown in the diagram. In practice the Queen acts on the advice of government ministers. Her main role today is a symbolic one which can unite the nation. She, and other members of the Royal Family, therefore undertake ceremonial duties such as greeting important visitors and recognising the completion of important projects.

However, the title is an inherited one rather than an elected one, and criticism is also made of the high cost of maintaining a monarchy. It seems likely that if the monarch does not attempt to enforce the theoretical power over the government, the widespread popularity of and interest in the Royal Family will continue. The monarch reigns but does not rule, and this makes a **republican** Britain unlikely.

PARLIAMENTARY TIME

Bills coming before Parliament fall into two main groups: government legislation and Private Members' Bills.

● *Government legislation* takes up the bulk of parliamentary time. At all stages the government of the day will try to ensure majority support for its proposals and the whip system is of major significance throughout. The Chief Whip is a member of the Cabinet and, with the help of the Assistant Whips, is responsible for ensuring support for the government by making sure that enough MPs turn up to vote in favour. The Opposition Whips will also be seeking maximum support from their members to oppose the government. Each party issues all its MPs with a daily letter showing the business of the day. Any matter which is underlined once requests attendance. If it is underlined twice, the Whip expects the member's attendance and support. A 'three-line whip' *demands* attendance and support. There are occasions when three-line whips are disobeyed: for example, in 1973 69 Labour MPs supported the Conservative Government's legislation for UK membership of the EEC, but such occurrences are rare and usually result in the offending MPs being disciplined. Normally the Chief Whip will seek an explanation for their voting behaviour and warn the MPs as to their future conduct. An MP who persistently votes against the party may 'have the whip withdrawn'. This means that he/she cannot attend Parliamentary party meetings and receives no help or information from the party. As a last resort he/she may not be selected to represent the party at the next General Election.

● *Private Members' Bills* are presented on certain Fridays in the session. There is always a ballot and those MPs coming at the top of the list have the greater chance of success.

Most of the remaining time in Parliament is taken up by adjournment debates, Question Time and Opposition Time.

● *Adjournment debates* normally occur in the last half-hour of the parliamentary day. By tradition a member of the House must propose that the day's business is ended and that the members may adjourn. Any backbencher may postpone the adjournment and in the process raise topical or urgent matters of concern. No legislation is possible but quite a bit of publicity can be got for individuals or groups. Members ballot for the privilege of raising matters at this time.

● *Question Time* allows members to support, examine and criticise the work of the various ministers. It is an opportunity to demand detailed answers from a minister and to critically examine his or her performance. All ministers, including the Prime Minister, have their share of Question Time. Questions are submitted two or three days in advance to give the minister time to prepare an answer. Often a seemingly innocent question brings an embarrassing supplementary question. If members only want information from a question they will ask for a written reply, but if their aim is to attract publicity to themselves or their cause they will prefer an oral answer.

● *Opposition time* There are 19 'supply' days each session which allow the Opposition to choose subjects for debate.

A whip

On Monday, 20th February, 1978, the House will meet at 2.30 p.m.

A Debate will take place on Nationalisation on a Government Motion and an Opposition amendment.

A good attendance throughout this debate is particuarly requested. A Division may take place and your attendance at 10 p.m. and until the Prayer is concluded is particularly requested, unless you have obtained a pair.

On Tuesday, 21st February, 1978, the House will meet at 2.30 p.m.

Conclusion of debate on Nationalisation. The Government may move a Guillotine motion.

There will be most important Divisions and your

attendance at 9.30 p.m. is essential.

James Falconer's Private Member's Bill

At the start of his second session in Parliament, James was lucky enough to have his name drawn in the ballot for Private Members' Bills. This gave him (and another nineteen MPs) the chance to introduce a Bill on one of twenty Fridays during the coming parliamentary session.

Since James had no idea what his Bill should be about, he asked a few of his more experienced backbench colleagues. 'You don't stand much chance', he was told by some. 'Pick a topic that'll be a vote-catcher. Something to give you a bit of good publicity.' Others said, 'This is your chance to act as an MP should. Make it a worthwhile Bill.'

14 The whip system

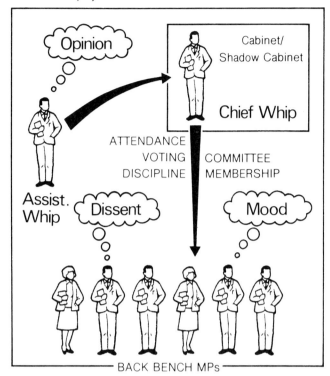

BACK BENCH MPs

James was a member of the Monday Club but he didn't think their ideas would carry the support of enough MPs.

Then the letters started coming in. People everywhere seemed to know that he had come high up on the ballot and his postbag bulged for weeks with letters from the Society to Prevent This and the Organisation Against That. They even came to his weekly surgeries, all these pressure groups. He did become interested in an idea suggested by the Newtown Working Mothers' Group: that employers should be obliged by law to supply nursery facilities if they employed more than 60 women.

James tried the idea out with a few MPs from all the major parties and got enough encouragement to have a civil servant draft his Bill. It had to be worded very carefully to avoid misunderstandings. The title of the bill became 'Nursery Provision for Children of Nursery-School Age Bill'.

The First Reading of the Bill–the formal one– was passed as there were hardly any MPs in the House that Friday, but for the Second Reading the place was packed and James was very nervous as he rose to make his prepared speech. The vote was very close, but on a free vote with no three-line whip it did get through. Now came the Committee Stage. Unfortunately for James and his Bill, several members of the Committee kept coming up with what

James thought were trifling complaints. Time was running out. Now he realised why only about 12% of Private Members' Bills are passed compared with 93% of government Bills. Unless. . . . He went to the Leader of the House to ask if he could use some of the government's time to make sure that the Bill got through the Committee Stage on to the Third Reading. He got a friendly letter back, but it said that although many government MPs were keen on the Bill it was too sensitive an issue to have this kind of government support, especially since many employers were complaining and saying how this was going to push up prices. The government was concerned to keep price increases down and he was sorry they could not help.

A few days later James was told that as it was near the end of session, there was no time left in the House for the Report Stage and so his Bill would not get through.

Questions

1. Where would Falconer and Brown sit in the House of Commons?
2. What is the function of each of the items labelled in the House of Commons photograph on page 12?
3. What are the main duties of the Speaker?
4. Why does the House of Commons have so many rules?

5. Give three possible reasons for the calling of a General Election.
6. Describe in detail how an idea can become a law.
7. What are the duties of the Opposition during this law-making process?
8. What are the duties of the Chief Whip?
9. What can the whips do to discipline an MP?
10. What opportunities does an MP have to speak in the House?
11. What efforts should James Falconer make to have his idea made law in the future?
12. Describe in detail who the people in photograph **11** on page 12 are and what they are doing.
13. Outline the duties of
    (a) the Lords,   (b) the monarch.

The Prime Minister and the Cabinet

The Prime Minister has appointed Peter Brown Secretary of State for Scotland. In order to understand his work and the work of the Cabinet it is first necessary to understand the principle of the separation of powers.

The Cabinet

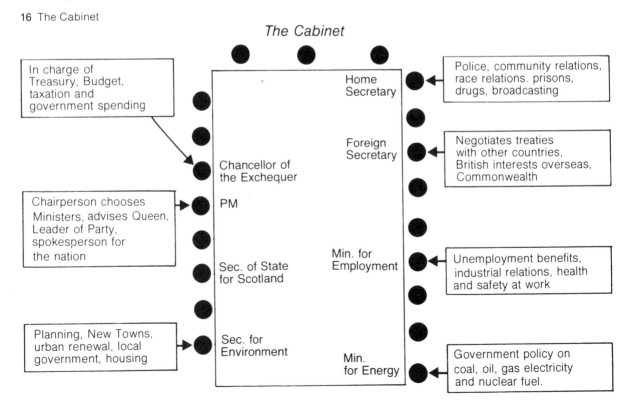

In charge of Treasury, Budget, taxation and government spending

Home Secretary

Police, community relations, race relations. prisons, drugs, broadcasting

Foreign Secretary

Negotiates treaties with other countries, British interests overseas, Commonwealth

Chancellor of the Exchequer

Chairperson chooses Ministers, advises Queen, Leader of Party, spokesperson for the nation

PM

Sec. of State for Scotland

Min. for Employment

Unemployment benefits, industrial relations, health and safety at work

Planning, New Towns, urban renewal, local government, housing

Sec. for Environment

Min. for Energy

Government policy on coal, oil, gas electricity and nuclear fuel.

Within the process of lawmaking and government, there are three different parts:

Separation of powers

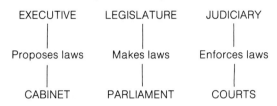

EXECUTIVE	LEGISLATURE	JUDICIARY
Proposes laws	Makes laws	Enforces laws
CABINET	PARLIAMENT	COURTS

● **The Executive** is the organ for policy decision making. It is the job of the Executive to carry out the government programme. (The Cabinet does not make the law. This is the function of Parliament. It can only suggest what it would like made law.)

● **The Legislature** is the organ responsible for law making. In the British system this is the function of Parliament. In theory, the House of Commons is supreme and controls the Executive and the judiciary.

● **The Judiciary** has the task of interpreting and implementing the law. It consists of the various levels of judges and is independent both of the Legislature and the Executive in that appointment is for life and is not dependent on any political party.

In the UK, the Executive is the Cabinet, which is composed of the Prime Minister (normally the leader of the majority party in the House of Commons or the leader of the party which can command a majority in the House), the Lord Chancellor and the senior ministers of the government. There is no set membership for the Cabinet; the total number of members, usually between twenty and twenty-five, is at the discretion of the Prime Minister. By convention, all members of Cabinet should be Members of Parliament and are responsible to Parliament.

The Prime Minister chairs the Cabinet and is responsible for all ministerial appointments, dismissals and reshuffles. The PM may be required to settle differences between government departments and to keep an eye on all important matters. The PM has to keep the Queen informed, nominate people for honours and appointments, and decide when to dissolve Parliament. The PM is regarded by the media, the public and the rest of the world as the leader and spokesperson for Britain.

The Cabinet is responsible for all government strategy, decision making and legislative proposals. All members of the Cabinet will take part in discussion, make proposals and participate in any vote. When a Cabinet decision is made every Cabinet minister is then bound by collective responsibility. This means they must publicly support the decision even if they were not in agreement. The alternative is to resign from the Cabinet.

Most ministers are in charge of a particular department of government (ministry): for example, the Department of Energy, the Exchequer or the Home Office, and have their own civil service department. The civil servants are all servants of the Crown. They are public employees who assist ministers to carry out their responsibilities.

Each minister is responsible to the Prime Minister, the Cabinet and to Parliament for the work and performance of his or her ministry. All government proposals with regard to the work of that department will be made by the Minister concerned, or by junior ministers. All major ministries have, in addition to the Minister, junior ministers of State who assist the Minister and who are normally responsible for particular areas of the Minister's department work.

The top civil servants will be in daily contact with their minister; they will present him or her with strategy papers and alternatives and will also be responsible for the administration of policies and legislation. Ministers are ultimately responsible to Parliament and will reply to both oral and written questions put by MPs. They take day to day decisions on the running of their department and are in charge of general strategy.

The Shadow Cabinet, appointed by the leader of the Opposition, has the task of criticising the work of the Cabinet ministers. A leading member of the Opposition becomes its spokesperson on a particular matter, for example, energy, and 'shadows' his/her opposite number in the government, being prepared to comment on his/her policies.

15 The civil service (servants of the Crown: non-political)

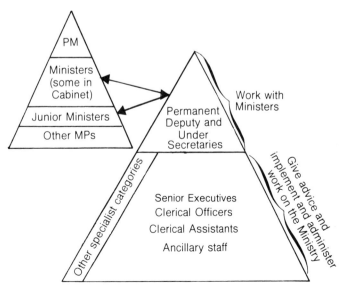

In recent years the appointment of MPs to serve on 14 Select Committees has increased the chances of more open government. Each ministerial department has a Select Committee which has the power to 'send for persons, papers and records' and therefore to question ministers and civil servants on the operation of their department. This enables Parliament to publicise faults and inefficiencies and to praise or condemn decisions. These Committees can also make recommendations, though departments can resist them if their ministers are prepared to defend their departments in the Commons.

Questions

1. List the people involved in each of the following: the Executive, the Legislature, the Judiciary.
2. Which Cabinet members would be most involved in a discussion on
   (a) police in Scotland;
   (b) the building of ships for the navy;
   (c) a cut in taxation?
3. In what ways does the civil service back up the work of Cabinet ministers?
4. What are the main duties of each of the following?
   (a) the Prime Minister;
   (b) the Shadow Cabinet;
   (c) the civil service;
   (d) Select Committees.
5. What is collective responsibility? Why does the Cabinet have this rule?

The Member of Parliament

WANTED: hard working individual, to work in cramped surroundings, on public business. Long hours, night work, no paid overtime. Weekdays at Westminster, weekends in constituency. Working holidays. Share secretary. £14 000 + secretarial allowance, postage and business phone calls. Help with travel. Canteen. Contract for five years maximum. Possible reappointment.

James Falconer, as a new Member of Parliament, is quickly learning the procedure and processes of Parliament. He is alread aware of many conflicting pressures on both his time and his loyalties. He recognises four main loyalties.

● *The national interest* must always be in his mind. He is aware of occasions on which some MPs have placed what they see as national interest above all else: for example, during the EEC debate (1973) and the devolution debate (1977–8).
● *His party* must normally command his support. He accepts that in the UK system most voters vote for parties rather than individuals and knows that he accepted his party's **manifesto** throughout his election campaign. The whips remind him of this.
● *His constituents* Both those who voted for and against him must be represented by him, although he insists that he is their **representative**, not their **delegate**.
● *His conscience* is of major importance, especially in matters of social legislation where he normally has a free vote: for example, issues such as capital punishment, abortion and euthanasia.

Clearly there will be occasions when his loyalties will conflict. If there is a matter of conscience which prevents him supporting his party he will inform the Chief Whip. Usually such an exercise of conscience will be accepted, but if it happens regularly then the party and the whip system will bring pressure to bear and may, as a last resort, discipline him.

His parliamentary day starts at 2.30 p.m., Monday to Thursday, and earlier on a Friday. There is no set time for the end of the parliamentary day, and debates have been known to last all night. Before 2.30 he has to sort out his mail, arrange replies where necessary, prepare his work for the day, research the issues due to be raised in the House, prepare any written or oral questions he may wish to ask, and be in contact with his parliamentary colleagues and the whips. From 2.30 onwards he will be in Parliament, which starts with the Speaker's procession and prayers. He may attend debates or be working outside the Chamber but available to vote in any division of the House, when he hears the Division Bell. As a Scottish Member of Parliament he attends the Scottish Grand Committee which deals with the committee stage of all Scottish Bills. He also has to prepare his maiden speech in the House. Traditionally it should be of modest length and non-controversial but it will be a valuable experience for future debates.

In addition to his parliamentary duties, James Falconer also has to attend to his constituency. As an MP elected from a highly marginal constituency, he must be very attentive to the needs and demands of his constituency. Every Friday during the parliamentary session he travels home to his Newtown constituency. He meets his election agent and discusses the business of the weekend. He will hold his 'surgery' on Saturday in the town hall. The

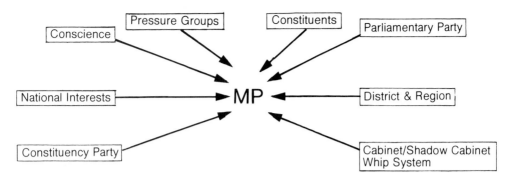

17 Pressures on MPs

surgery is advertised in the local paper and gives his constituents the opportunity to raise matters of concern to them personally. The matters they raise may require Mr Falconer to contact a local authority, or a national body, such as the Vehicle Licensing Centre, on their behalf. It may, however, be a subject which he will wish to raise in the House of Commons at Question Time.

As the local MP he is also occupied most weekends in political, social and charitable engagements. These might include party meetings, talks, party and town social events, the opening of fêtes,and interviews with the local press and television. This keeps him in the public eye and raises his popularity. On Sunday night he returns to London for another parliamentary week.

A day in the life of James Falconer MP

8.00	Read selection of newspapers
9.00	Read mail, answer as many letters as possible
10.00	Meeting with pressure group
11.00	Parliamentary Party meeting
11.30	Backbench 1922 Committee meeting
1.00	Lunch with local newspaper reporter
2.30	Speaker's procession and prayers
2.45	Question Time: put question on constituent's problem; be ready with Supplementary
3.45	Ministerial statement on fishing policy
4.00	Orders of the day: debate on unemployment Two-line whip on divisions
7.00	Possible emergency debate
10.00	Adjournment debate

It can be hard for an MP, particularly a hardworking one whose constituency is not near London, to have much time left for a personal life. This letter from Peter Brown's wife shows some of the pressures on an MP's family.

Aviemore, Tuesday

Dear Peter

The kids and I are enjoying our break. What a pity you couldn't join us! You really should try to take a few days off, you know — all MPs work too hard — and I don't want you to get ill.

Before I left, Mrs C from round the corner came by wanting you to do something about her son's grant for university. I gave her a note of when your surgery was, so that you can deal with it. The queue of constituents will be even longer than usual this week.

You'll really have to get some more notices about the surgery printed — I'm not an information service!

You'll have heard that James Falconer has had to take on more staff in his estate agent's office. He really can't hope to do two jobs. Perhaps if his business was in London he might manage, but only being here at weekends, and having all the constituency work to do then, is almost impossible. Mind you, it could be said that you have two jobs too — being an MP and a Cabinet Minister. I used to think we hardly saw you when you were just an MP. Now the only time we see you is when you're on TV, or behind a mountain of red Dispatch boxes! I think Meg Falconer is getting really fed up with seeing so little of James. She has to deal with everything in the business as well as being mother and father to the kids during the week. No wonder there are so many divorces in MPs' families!

We'll be back home in time to meet you off the London plane on Friday afternoon. Let's hope the garden fête doesn't last too long on Saturday — you really must visit your mother this weekend. And please try to leave your papers in London — sometimes I think I'll have to turn up at your surgery to get to speak to you!

Love,

Jean

Questions

1. What things would encourage you to apply for the job of MP? What would put you off?
2. What can an MP do to make his/her day less busy?
3. Write a letter from Peter to his wife Jean answering some of the points raised.
4. Why do each of the pressures on MPs influence them? Give examples.
5. What part does a surgery play in democracy?

2. Political Issues

In studying Parliament and government we must look at major issues which arise. In these pages we look at several matters of national and constitutional importance.

Executive versus Legislature

In theory the elected House of Commons is supreme. In practice, the system has developed in such a way that the Executive (Cabinet) increasingly dominates the Legislature (Commons). Cabinet business demands most of Parliament's time and the statistics show that its legislative success is much greater than that of the ordinary MP. Even in the nineteenth century, Disraeli could demand of his supporters, 'Damn your principles, sir, stick to your party!' and it is undoubtedly true that most members of the Commons are loyal to and support their party.

Why is it that Mr Brown and his Cabinet colleagues can expect support? Why will Mr Falconer be inclined to support his party on most occasions?

The reasons lie in an electoral system that has consistently produced two major political parties in terms of parliamentary voting strength. The two-party system led to a strong party discipline expressed in the whip system. Ordinary MPs are also faced with the following pressures:

(a) The British electorate tend to vote for a party rather than an individual, so MPs' parliamentary careers will depend, at least in part, on their party and constituency continuing to accept them as their representative and candidate.
(b) If MPs are members of the Government, they know that defeat on a vote of confidence could mean a General Election which their party might lose.
(c) The two-party system heightens party conflict and for MPs to vote against their party or even to abstain may be interpreted as giving support to the Opposition.
(d) If the matter at issue was contained in their party's election **manifesto**, MPs would be expected to give their support and their vote.
(e) MPs who are keen to achieve promotion know that one yardstick will be their loyalty to the party and its legislative proposals.

MPs are however, not totally without influence. At parliamentary party meetings they will have an opportunity to air their points of view, but if they are minority ones they will be expected to accept the majority view. They can also inform the whips of any dissatisfaction. In 1969, a large group of Labour MPs used this method to end any possibility of the Labour Government introducing **industrial relations** legislation, which they saw as being against the interest of trade unions, based on the document 'In Place of Strife'. As a last resort, the MP can abstain or vote against any proposal. The fact that this a rare occurrence is a demonstration of the power of the Executive.

Questions

1. What is meant by the 'two-party system'?
2. Under what circumstances will an MP vote along party lines? Are there any circumstances in which an MP might vote against the party?
3. What chance do ordinary MPs have to let the government know that they are against an Executive decision?

Nationalism and Devolution

Although the United Kingdom is ruled for the most part from Westminster, there have, from time to time, been demands from parts of the Kingdom that more power should be taken from the centre and devolved to Northern Ireland, Scotland and Wales.

In Northern Ireland, violence has broken out repeatedly as the two main sections of the community have disagreed over who should rule there. In 1972, a period of direct rule from Westminster replaced previous attempts at devolved power through a Northern Ireland Government. Since then, politicians both in the House of Commons and in Northern Ireland have tried to find a form of devolved government which would be acceptable to both sides of the community. Plans for an Assembly have been drawn and redrawn, and elections have been held, but the people of Northern Ireland do not yet agree as to how they should be ruled.

In Scotland and Wales the rise in popularity of Nationalist parties in the late 1960s encouraged the major parties to move towards a commitment to some form of devolved government for Scotland and Wales. The main reasons for the rise of the SNP in Scotland were a growing disenchantment with centralised and remote government; a protest vote against the two-party system; an increasing criticism of Labour and Conservative Governments and their apparent inability to satisfy the economic and social needs of the country; the discovery of North Sea Oil which offered salvation for the Scottish economy if it was, as was claimed, 'Scotland's oil'.

In 1979, the people of Scotland and Wales were given the opportunity in a **referendum** to say whether or not they were in favour of an Assembly for their part of the UK. In Scotland, the Assembly, to be set up in Edinburgh, would have 150 elected members who would have the power to make laws for Scotland in areas such as health, social work, schools, housing, planning, criminal and civil law, shop hours and local government. A controversial clause in the Scotland Act (1978) said that 40% of those eligible to vote in the referendum would have to vote 'Yes'. The result of the vote was that 33% voted 'Yes' for a Scottish Assembly, and 30% voted 'No'. Since 37% had not voted this meant that although the 'Yes' vote won a narrow victory, it did not reach the required 40%. (In Wales, the vote was 12% Yes, 47% No.)

Since 1979, commitments have been made by all major parties to look at the idea of **devolution** again

for Scotland, but in the meantime Scotland continues to be run from Westminster and from the Scottish Office.

The Secretary of State for Scotland, a member of the Cabinet, is responsible in Scotland for some work which is done in England and Wales by the Home Secretary and the Ministers of Agriculture, Transport, Social Services and the Environment. He or she is also responsible for the Scottish educational and legal systems. The Scottish Secretary is assisted by junior ministers and by civil servants in the Scottish Office in Edinburgh. Five departments carry out the administration of the Secretary's responsiblities: Agriculture and Fisheries, Development, Economic Planning, Education, Home and Health.

The Scottish Grand Committee, composed of all Scottish MPs plus enough other MPs to reflect the party balance in the House of Commons, considers all Scottish Bills which pass through the Commons.

It is generally agreed that the Secretary of State has to control a wide range of decision making, without having sufficient independence to take decisions without reference to the British Cabinet and Government. The political differences between Scotland and the rest of the UK can make Scotland

19 First meeting of Scottish Grand Committee with members of SNP demonstrating outside

harder to govern, particularly since Scotland regularly votes Labour while the rest of Britain may change between electing a Labour and a Conservative government. A Conservative Scottish Secretary can be expected to have a harder time than a Labour one.

Questions

1. What does devolution mean to people in (a) Northern Ireland and (b) Scotland?
2. Explain the rise in popularity of the SNP in Scotland in the late 1960s and 1970s.
3. Why do supporters of devolution claim that the 40% rule was unfair?
4. To what extent do each of the following give Scotland a separate form of government:
   (a) Secretary of State for Scotland,
   (b) Scottish Office,
   (c) Scottish Grand Committee.

The European Dimension

In 1973, the Conservative Government led Britain into the European Community. In 1975, the new Labour Government organised a referendum, and the majority of voters chose to remain in the EEC. As a member of the EEC, Britain is now involved in and affected by the major bodies who run the Community.

The Council of Ministers

Each government sends a minister to the council. Normally it is the Foreign Secretary, but, for particular topics, the minister most directly concerned is sent; for example, the Minister for Agriculture when the Common Agricultural Policy is being discussed. The Council is a decision-making body. If there is a difference of opinion a weighted majority is necessary to reach a decision. However, on very important issues, a unanimous vote is required.

The European Commission

Fourteen commissioners, of which two are British, are appointed by national governments, but they are not members of that government. Each commissioner is given charge of one area of the Community's responsibility: for example, transport or agriculture. Their main task is to work out policy, which is then sent to the European Parliament and then to the Council of Ministers.

20 The European Parliament

The European Parliament

A total of 434 Euro-MPs are directly elected every five years (since 1979) by the electorate of each country. Britain has the right to elect 81 members representing 81 Euro-constituencies. This Parliament is consulted on and debates all major policy issues. It has the power to refuse to accept the annual budget presented to it by the Commission.

Opponents of Britain's membership of the European Community are concerned that Britain is now bound by rules and decisions made in Brussels which can be binding on Britain. Our national government, therefore, is tied to the principle of common policies in, for example, transport, agriculture and fisheries, taxation, and trade. It can be argued that our sovereignty or freedom to run our own affairs is restricted.

Supporters of membership argue that the limitations on freedom are minor, and that the benefits of membership more than make up for any loss of sovereignty.

When direct elections were first held to the European Parliament in 1979, it was hoped that this part of the EEC would be strengthened. The British public would be able to consult their Euro-MPs and this in turn would give them more power to argue their case. However, much of the publicity in recent years has centred on the conflict between various national governments and the Community decision-makers. Aspects of policy have conflicted with what different governments see as the best interests of the EEC and of themselves. For example, Britain has argued over the size of the contribution it is expected to make to EEC funds; and there have been disagreements over 'unfair trading' between countries.

An argument which is unlikely to be resolved is between those who see membership of the Community as an advantage in that there is the possibility of closer links both economically and politically. Others regard this as intervention in the affairs of an individual country and an unnecessary extra tier of government.

Questions

1. What part does Britain play in each of the three main institutions of the European Community?
2. What are the advantages and disadvantages of closer political links between Britain and other EEC countries?

Representation in Parliament

MPs are elected to the House of Commons to represent their constituents. It might be reasonable to assume, therefore, that MPs are a mirror of British society, with a mixture of age, occupations, races and sexes which reflects that of society as a whole. However, most MPs are male, most are middle aged, most come from 'middle-class' occupations like the law and business, and all are white. Many people are concerned that such an unrepresentative group of people cannot represent the views of the British people adequately.

The black community is particularly concerned at its total lack of national representation. In 1979, there were five black parliamentary candidates; in 1983, there were 17, but none gained a seat out of 650. There are black councillors at local government level, but it seems there will have to be more black candidates and a greater push to get black voters to vote for there to be greater representation at national level, as well as an effort to overcome the prejudice of white voters against black candidates.

Although more than half the population of the country is female, in the 1983 election, only 23 out of 650 MPs were female. Many important Committees of the House of Commons have no women on them, even ones which are particularly to do with aspects of women's lives. Although large numbers of women are members of political parties, few are selected as prospective candidates. The 300 Group works towards helping more women into decision-making areas of political and public life (onto committees, Parent Teacher Associations, local government), encourages the political parties to choose capable women for important posts and tries to publicise the under-representation of more than half of the population.

As MPs speak for their constituents in Parliament, they might be expected to share the views of most of their constituents. Yet, opinion polls, which question a sample of the population on important issues, repeatedly show big differences of opinion on some important issues. For example, each time the reintroduction of capital punishment has been debated in the House of Commons, the motion has been defeated, yet opinion polls show that the majority of the general public favour its reintroduction. Other issues such as policies on the National Health Service, defence, and education show a similar gap between what MPs think and what the public think.

People who want their views known widely and want to influence government policy often join together to form a pressure group. Some pressure groups have sympathetic MPs to speak out for them. Others make their views known by lobbying, meeting MPs to talk about their worries and concerns. But the biggest pressure groups with the biggest financial backing can afford to be more active, do more lobbying, and be more effective as persuaders. The trade unions, operating as a pressure group, sponsor Labour MPs, paying some of their election expenses in return for support in the House of Commons. This makes sure their views are known, perhaps to a greater extent than the public would agree to.

However, it is a central point of British politics that MPs are not delegates simply doing what their constituents tell them to do. MPs may have inside knowledge, or a deeper understanding of the issue. Thus they represent the interest of their constituents as *they* see these interests. MPs do what they consider is best for the voters: if the voters don't like what has been done, they can vote for someone else at the next election.

Questions

1. Explain why the House of Commons might be said not to represent fairly each of the following: women; blacks; the young; the working class.
2. What are the arguments for and against allowing MPs to vote on an issue as they think rather than as their constituents would wish them to vote?

3. Local Government

Central government makes policy decisions and organises things like defence for the country as a whole. Local government, on the other hand, carries out policy decisions at a local level and runs services best organised on a smaller scale. Local government can identify locally the needs and problems of the individual citizen; it can offer citizens the opportunity to participate in the business of government; and it can keep a check on central government.

Local **authorities**, although elected democratically, do not decide for themselves what power and responsibilities they have. These are laid down by Act of Parliament, and can be changed.

In the mid-1970s new structures of local government were introduced in England, Wales and Scotland. Table 21 shows the break-down of responsibilities within the various levels of local government. The new structures had four main aims for the news authorities:

● *Power:* local government should have greater responsibilities and be less dependent on central government.

● *Effectiveness:* every local government service should operate on a scale which would allow high standards, good value for money and greater efficiency.

● *Local democracy:* locally elected bodies should be genuinely in charge of the local situation and responsible to the local electorate.

● *Local involvement:* people should be brought into the process of reaching decisions.

By examining the structure of local government in Scotland we can see how far these aims have been met.

Local Government in Scotland

Scotland is divided into nine Regions, which are the first tier of the structure. Each Region is sub-divided into Districts. In total there are fifty-three District Councils. (There are also three multi-purpose Island Authorities outwith the two-tier system. These are in Orkney, Shetland and the Western Isles.) The

21   Who does what?

	Responsible for:
England	
(1) **Metropolitan areas**	
6 Metropolitan County Councils	Overall planning, transport, police, fire services, waste disposal
36 District Councils	Education, personal social services, housing, local planning, environmental health, leisure, waste collection
(2) **London**	
Greater London Council	Overall planning, transport, fire, some housing, waste disposal
Inner London Education Authority	Education in inner London (12 boroughs plus City of London)
32 London Borough Councils and city of London	Housing, local planning, environmental heath, education (in 20 outer boroughs), personal social services, waste collection
	0(3) **Non-metropolitan areas**
39 'shire' County Councils	Overall planning, transport, police, fire services, education, personal social services, waste disposal
296 District Councils	Housing, local planning, environmental health, leisure, waste collection
Over 8000 local (i.e. parish and town) councils	Local amenities
Wales	
8 County Councils	Much the same as non-metropolitan England
37 District Councils	Ditto
About 500 community councils	Local amenities
Scotland	
9 Regional Councils	Overall planning, transport, police, fire services, education, personal social services, waste disposal, water, drains
53 District Councils	Housing, local planning, environmental health, leisure, tourism, waste collection
Over 1200 Community Councils	Local amenities
3 Island Councils	All regional and district powers

Northern Ireland is not covered in this brief. Most functions there are conducted by central government or its appointees.

(Source: *The Economist*, 19 November 1983)

number of Districts per Region, and the populations of each Region are given below.

Region	Districts	Population (1981)
Borders	4	99 248
Central	3	273 078
Dumfries and Galloway	4	145 078
Fife	3	326 480
Grampian	5	470 596
Highland	8	200 030
Lothian	4	735 892
Strathclyde	19	2397 827
Tayside	3	391 529

The overall plan is that the functions of local government can best be allocated to one of two levels of authority. The District is clearly more concerned with local matters, while the Region is responsible for services requiring planning and administration over a larger geographical area. Some services are shared jointly by the two tiers: for example, museums and galleries, and recreation. The decision to have multi-purpose Island Authorities was a recognition of the distinct geographic and social character of these islands.

In addition to the two main tiers, Community Councils were set up. Any community can choose to form an elected Community Council. It has no statutory powers, but is a vehicle for expressing local views and taking local action. The overall responsibility for the setting up of such Councils with codes of procedure and arrangments for elections is that of the Island or District Authorities. These Community Councils may raise funds, and receive special project grants. They can also expect help–money, staff and facilities–from Regional, Island or District Councils.

Finance

The services which local government provides are financed from three main sources: rates; government **grants**; charges and borrowing.

● *Rates*. A tax is paid to the local authority on all buildings within its boundary. Every building, shop, house, cinema, factory has a rateable value. The rateable value worked out for each property depends on several factors such as size and type of property and location. This system allows an

Scotland
Regions and Regional headquarters

■ Island Authorities

1 Inverness	2 Aberdeen	3 Dundee	4 Glenrothes
5 Stirling	6 Glasgow	7 Edinburgh	8 Dumfries
9 Newton St Boswells			

22 Scotland: Regions and Regional headquarters

authority to allocate a greater rateable value to business premises than houses, and to larger houses than smaller ones.

The rates are calculated as follows: the authority adds up the total rateable value for all properties in its area. It also calculates its total **expenditure** for the year. It subtracts the money it will receive from other sources. The amount left has to be raised from the rates.

This amount is divided by the total rateable value to produce the rate for every pound of rateable value. Each owner of property can then be told how much to pay in rates in a year. For example:

Total rateable value	=	£30 700 000

Total expenditure	=	£69 851 675
Money from other sources	=	£28 431 710

Amount to be raised from rates	=	£41 419 965

$$\text{Rate} = \frac{41\,419\,965}{30\,700\,000} = £1.35$$

Therefore a property with a rateable value of £75 will pay £(75 × 1.35) = £101 in that year.

These rates are calculated both by the Regional and the District Authorities. Therefore the rates which a property owner pays are made up of both a Regional and a District rate.

23 Functions of local authorities in Scotland

● *Rate Support Grant.* Central Government gives every local authority a certain amount of money from the Exchequer to help pay for **services** and keep the rates down. Other grants are given for specific purposes: for example, Urban Aid.

● *Charges and borrowing.* Charges are made for the provision of some local services and may cover all or some of the costs of providing the service. These may include rents for council housing, payments for public transport, payment for some school meals, charges towards use of services such as parks, museums, community education, etc. Money is also borrowed from people who can invest in a local authority to get a rate of interest just as they can invest in a public company.

Many people believe that the rates system is in need of reform. As it stands, a household, which consists

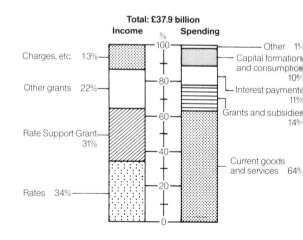

24 Local authority finance 1983–4
(Source: *The Economist*, 19 November 1983)

of a couple with five children and only one person working, would pay the same amount in rates as another family (living next door in the same kind of house) which consists of both earning, and five children, three of whom work and live at home. However, alternatives such as a local income tax or a local sales tax would be difficult to introduce and operate.

Criticisms and Problems

CENTRAL VERSUS LOCAL GOVERNMENT

Local government depends on central government for its powers and for more than half of its finance, as Fig. 24 shows. Therefore central government is likely at times to interfere with local government when their aims do not coincide.

If central government has a national policy of cutting back on public spending, it will want to make sure that local authorities play their part in this policy by cutting back on the services which they provide. The local authority, on the other hand, may feel that it was elected to provide these services, and may not wish to co-operate with central government. For example, a local authority may feel that, in order to continue its policy of relieving great poverty and multiple deprivation within its area, it must spend on housing improvement and social services. It may therefore feel that cuts in services would mean severe hardship to many people. But central government might insist that cutbacks must be made somewhere. It might suggest targets for spending in each authority and tie future spending levels to successful reductions in current ones. Local governments who 'overspend' would therefore be threatened with having their government grants cut back even further the following year. And central government might not allow them to increase the rates to bridge the gap between income and spending. The criticism is made that since local authorities are democratically elected locally to carry out policies put before the electorate, they should be allowed to get on with these policies. Central government should not interfere with this local democracy. On the other hand, central government is also democratically elected to run the whole country, and the national needs are more important than any local needs. The conflict at times between these two layers of democracy remains unresolved.

PAYMENT OF COUNCILLORS

Unlike MPs, local government councillors are not paid a salary. They receive expenses, and are usually paid by their employer if they have to be absent from work on council business. Many people argue that nowadays it requires full-time councillors to run local authorities and that therefore they should be paid. It is possible that more highly experienced and able people might stand as councillors if a salary was paid, and that they would be able to devote all their energies to council business. However, others feel that a good councillor is someone who has a commitment to the local area and is prepared to work hard with no financial reward.

COMMITTEES

Local authorities have to control a huge volume of services. Therefore, many decisions require the go-ahead of the elected councillors. A committee system is used to spread the workload, and small groups of councillors can specialise in and deal with particular departments. For example, a Scottish Region will have (among others) a Social Work Committee, and a District Council will have a Housing Committee. The criticism is made that much decision making in vital areas of policy goes on in small committees, with the full council being used only as a rubber stamp.

DEMOCRACY

With local governments, voters are now faced with several layers of people who represent them. There are Community Councils, District and Regional Councils, central government and the European Parliament. In the face of all this representation, voters have not become any less apathetic than they used to be about local democracy. The turnout at local elections is still disappointing compared with the turnout at national elections. Often, too, voters cast their vote in local elections, not on the basis of local issues, but as a criticism of the way national parties are behaving. Certainly the mass media uses the results of local elections as a kind of cheap opinion poll of national politics. However, although coverage of local issues relies very heavily on local newspapers, there are occasions when the local community is aroused by a local issue and registers its view through the election of local councillors.

Community Views Rejected

Last night at a stormy meeting of the Glenforth District Council's Housing Committee, Councillor Cunningham refused to accept the proposals of the Glenforth Central Community Council for the development of twenty houses for single people on vacant land, and instead accepted the recommendation of Councillor Jones that no action should be taken until the Planning and Development Committee and the Finance Committee of the Regional Council meet next month.

Fred Johnston, Chairman of the Central Community Council, said of the District Council today, 'They are more interested in their expenses than in local improvements, that lot. Always delaying decisions saying they need approval from the Region or Government. It's a piece of nonsense. Last month it was education they said they couldn't touch because it was the Region's business. I know for a fact that the District Council are responsible for housing – but now they say that money comes from the Region and everything is part of the Region's plan. Where do the ordinary people of Glenforth fit into all this – that's what I want to know.'

Councillor Cunningham, on his way to work today, explained that, though the District Council is in charge of certain services, the Regional Council has overall control of what happens within the whole region. He denied charges of holding meetings to make money: 'We get a flat rate attendance allowance and travelling expenses. Oh, and something for food. Quote me on that!'

Questions

1. Why do we have local government?
2. What are the duties of a Community Council?
3. To which councillor (Regional or District) would you go if you wished to complain about: pollution of the air; a hole in the road; dirty water; housing; dustmen; schools; noise from a pub; an old-age pensioner in need of help?
4. Describe the different sources of local government revenue. What other ways might there be of raising money?
5. What right does central government have to intervene in the affairs of a local authority?
6. What can central government do if a local authority resists the ideas of central government?
7. What are the arguments for and against the payment of local councillors?
8. Why do local authorities delegate much of their work to committees?
9. Why might many voters become apathetic about local government?
10. What problems does Glenforth Community Council have?

25 The Community Council

4. The Mass Media

In any society the mass **media** play a significant and influential role. They have been described as the 'Fourth Estate' after the Houses of Lords and Commons, the People and the Church. Press, radio and television share similar functions:

● To *inform* on news ranging from the local to international.
● To *educate* by providing information in a structured manner. In addition, both radio and television provide school and university education programmes.
● To *entertain*. Newspapers entertain by providing articles, features and cartoons. Radio and television have an obligation to provide a balanced programme of entertainment, including drama, films and the arts.
● To *persuade* and *influence*. The most obvious attempt to influence is through advertising. Less obviously, each newspaper has a political standpoint which it wishes to convey to the reader.

By Acts of Parliament, television and radio are supposed to ensure that a proper balance of views is expressed. Therefore, although individuals and political parties can express political views through these mediums, these will be balanced by the views of others. This applies not only to party political broadcasts but also to documentaries, discussion programmes, etc.

Newspapers
PRESENTATION OF NEWS

Since the main aim of a newspaper is to sell as many papers as possible, the way it presents its news must be attractive to its readers. Newspaper owners seem to aim their newspapers at one of two different types of reader: one who wants a lot of information presented in a straightforward way, and who is interested in politics, **industry** and business (a reader of the 'quality' paper); and one who wants the most important bits of information but also wants a lot of entertainment (a reader of the 'popular' paper). Since some people buy both types of paper there is no such thing as a typical 'quality' reader or a typical 'popular' reader.

Every quality newspaper will not have the same characteristics and every popular newspaper will not be identical. Each newspaper has its own style. But there are, nevertheless, some common features of each broad type.

26 The difference in content and presentation between quality and popular newspapers

Characteristic	Quality	Popular
Size	Broadsheet	Tabloid
Photographs	Few	Many
News stories	Politics, business, foreign affairs, sport	Mainly human interest but also most important events
Language	Often difficult to read	Simple, short sentences, easy to read
Headlines	Long, explanatory	Short, snappy
Background articles	Informative on important issues	'Secret confessions', sometimes simplified explanation of Budget, etc.
Magazine elements	Reviews of theatre, books, films, fashion, crosswords	Crosswords, pinups, articles on pop stars, and footballers, gossip page, competitions

How the same news story is presented by a popular paper and a quality paper

The political views of the newspaper owners and editors are apparent in a number of ways. The editorial will state the paper's views on significant political, social and economic events, and will criticise the activities of people who do not share the paper's views. While the editors do not deliberately wish to deceive their readers, they do make sure that what they think of as important news gets prominent coverage. Thus an article can appear on the front page of one paper with a banner headline, and at the bottom of an inside page in another paper with a different political view. Photographs can be particularly powerful and influential, especially in the run-up to elections. If an editor wishes people to think a candidate untrustworthy, an unflattering photograph can be chosen. Another candidate can be shown making a forceful speech to an admiring audience. By careful choice of photographs, and the subtle way many stories are handled, newspapers can influence readers' views, not only on political matters, but on issues like the role of women, race relations, crime, and disarmament.

The type of advertising appearing in each newspaper also varies. An advertiser is aiming for a particular market and therefore a particular type of newspaper reader: a supermarket advert is more likely to appear in a popular paper, and an advert for an airline company in a quality paper read by business people.

As well as grouping newspapers as popular or quality, there are daily or weekly papers; morning or evening papers; local, provincial or national papers.

JIMMY'S SWEET MOMENT

Handsome local MP, James Falconer, brought the house down yesterday when he kissed Betty McFadden (65), winner of the garden fête's sweet-making competition. Said Betty, a grandmother of four, 'He doesn't need any of my sweets, he's sweet enough already.'

After his speech opening the fête, James and his beautiful young wife, who wore a turquoise silk dress and matching feather hat spent the afternoon touring the stalls with the Rev. Williamson, an old schoolfriend of Mr Falconer.

During his visit Mr Falconer spoke to stallholders many of whom are customers of his estate agency in the town.

As they left, Mrs Falconer was presented with a bouquet of red roses by Patricia Williamson (5), daughter of the Rev. Williamson.

Local MP promises action for working mothers

James Falconer made an important speech yesterday when he opened St Jude's Garden Fête, which may give a hint as to the subject he will choose for his Private Member's Bill later this session. He commented on the increasing number of nursery places needed in the constituency because of the recently opened factories employing women. He said, 'In this age of equality, I believe it to be the right of every woman to go out to work. Without sufficient nursery places in the are the married women in th constituency are at a disa vantage. I intend to everything in my power make it illegal for a authority to have fewer n sery places than the numb of nursery school-age ch dren in its area.'

Mr Falconer and his w spent the afternoon at t fête, which was held in aid churches in West Africa, cause which Mrs Falcor has worked for in the pas

PRODUCING A PAPER

The organisation of a newspaper can be divided into three main phases: collection; editing and presentation; production and distribution.

● *Collection* Written news reports are presented by staff reporters, freelance reporters, foreign correspondents, etc. Articles and news items are also written up from stories sent in by news agencies such as Reuters, Press Association and Extel. Added to this is information on the weather, television and radio programmes, classified advertisements, as well as feature articles and special interest pages.

Visual material – photographs, cartoons and other graphics – have also to be collected.

● *Editing and presentation* Major newspapers have editors in charge of news, foreign affairs, sport, features, etc. Their task is to decide on the final length of reports and to check on their accuracy. Sub-editors write up received stories to the correct length.

The Editor-in-Chief decides on the general attitude of the newspaper, and this policy will be reflected in the contents of the paper. One of the Editor's tasks is to write the editorial, where the view of the newspaper on a major news item is given. The Editor also takes decisions on the final layout of the paper, especially the front page.

● *Production and distribution* All articles are typeset, sometimes using a computer, and printed. They are then distributed to newspaper sellers and newsagents.

OWNERSHIP

Most national newspapers are owned by a few large publishing groups, most of which also have interests in other branches of the media, such as **commercial** television, commercial radio and magazines. Some of these groups are, in turn, owned by larger organisations.

The fewer newspapers there are, the greater chance there is of only a few points of view being represented. Where there is a danger of a group having a **monopoly** in the media, because of takeover or bankruptcy, the matter can be referred to the Monopolies and Mergers Commission. This includes cases where newspaper owners may have an interest in owning commercial television and/or radio stations. In this way it is hoped that a wide range of opinions will be made known to the public.

27 National newspapers

	Title and foundation date	Controlled by	Circulation (average Jan.–June 1983)
National dailies			
'Populars'	*Daily Express* (1900)	Fleet Holdings	1 889 995
	Daily Mail (1896)	Associated Newspapers Group	1 806 022
	Daily Mirror (1903)	Pergamon Press	3 315 070
	Daily Star (1978)	Fleet Holdings	1 337 486
	Morning Star (1966)	The People's Press Printing Society	29 847
	The Sun (1964)	News International	4 170 909
'Qualities'	*The Daily Telegraph* (1855)	Telegraph Newspaper Trust	1 266 069
	Financial Times (1888)	Pearson Longman	215 570
	The Guardian (1821)	The Guardian and Manchester Evening News	437 222
	The Times (1785)	News International	336 189
National Sundays			
'Populars'	*The Mail on Sunday* (1982)	Associated Newspapers Group	1 307 060
	News of the World (1843)	News International	4 074 424
	Sunday Express (1918)	Fleet Holdings	2 616 825
	Sunday Mirror (1963)	Pergamon Press	3 512 228
	Sunday People (1881)	Pergamon Press	3 392 746
'Qualities'	*The Observer* (1791)	George Outram & Co.	783 068
	Sunday Telegraph (1961)	Telegraph Newspaper Trust	738 193
	Sunday Times (1822)	News International	1 288 448

Britain Handbook 1984

LIMITATIONS

Although Britain enjoys what could loosely be described as 'freedom of the press' there are certain limitations imposed on newspapers.

● *The law of libel*   Like ordinary people in Britain, newspapers must ensure that they do not publish a statement which is defamatory, i.e. which brings a person into hatred, fear, ridicule or contempt. A lawyer is normally employed to check that the newspaper is not likely to be sued for libel.

● *Sub-judice rules*   During a trial, newspapers cannot comment in a way which might prejudice the fairness of the case. If the court considers that this has happened, then the newspaper could be held to be in contempt of court.

● *Official Secrets Acts* (1899, 1911, 1920)   These were introduced to prevent the publication of information from official sources which could endanger the country.

● *'D' Notices*   There is also a body called the Services, Press and Broadcasting Committee, which, on the advice of government, gives guidance to journalists on what can be published.

● *Other Acts of Parliament*   Newspapers must abide by laws in the same way as citizens. Examples of relevant laws are the Race Relations Act and the Sex Discrimination Act. There are also specific laws which affect advertising and some legal proceedings.

● *'Laws' of morality*   Many of these are not laws but conventions and are likely to change gradually.

● *The Press Council*   Unlike the other restraints mentioned, the Press Council has no legal authority. Newspapers accept that it will monitor their activities, as it has done since it was reconstitued in 1963. Its main aims are to deal with complaints by the public and to protect the freedom and reputation of the Press.

● *Public taste*   Newspapers are in business to make money and they can only do this if they sell as many copies as possible. Therefore, although at times they do try to shape public views, they are also attempting to reflect them. Editors must be guided by what they think their readers wish to see in their newspaper.

The Future of the *Daily Graphic*

Charlie Todd was not looking forward to the meeting with the owner, Lord Southfield. Sales of the *Daily Graphic* had dropped alarmingly in the last year, and he knew that, as Editor, he was going to have to take some of the blame. He could not say it was all because of competition from television and the new commercial radio station. For some reason the circulation figures for his main rival, the *Morning Clarion,* were rising steadily. Mind you, they had a woman's supplement every day and a special colour magazine on Saturdays, so Charlie supposed these must be part of the attraction. But how did they manage to balance the books when his own showed that for each paper sold, there was a loss of one penny?

	Cost per copy (pence)
Wages of reporters, printers, etc.	5.1
Paper, ink, etc.	9.0
Rates and rent	0.6
Power	0.4
Advertising	2.0
Distribution	2.7
Administration	1.2
	21.0

	Income per copy (pence)
Sales of newspaper	12.0
Advertising in newspaper	8.0
	20.0

There were many things which the *Daily Graphic* had tried in the last couple of years. They had invested in new machinery – the very latest computer techniques (where did Lord Southfield get the money?) – and they had even persuaded the various chapels (or unions) to accept that at least some of the surplus workers would not be replaced. All this had been accompanied by the launching of a new style of *Daily Graphic* – they had gone over to tabloid – much more appealing to most people; they had kept the price of the paper below that of most of their competitors; they had even advertised on television. What they needed was a sensational scoop which could run for a few days so that new readers would stay with the paper.

One thing was for sure. Lord Southfield wasn't going to keep subsidising his beloved *Graphic* with the money from his successful hotels for ever. It looked like a shut-down . . . permanently. And who would employ the ex-Editor of a bankrupt paper?

Questions

1. What are the main functions of the Press?
2. What are the main differences between a popular paper and a quality paper?
3. Comment on the different styles of reporting in the two articles on James Falconer's visit to the fête.
4. In what ways can a newspaper show its support for a particular political viewpoint?
5. List the steps which a news item takes from the event to its appearance on the front page.
6. What are the duties of the Editor-in-Chief?
7. Make a table of the newspapers in Table **27** in order of popularity. Use the following headings: newspaper; controller; circulation; style (popular/quality).
8. What sort of articles and news items must a newspaper be careful not to print?
9. If a newspaper was losing money, as the *Daily Graphic* was, what efforts could it make to improve its financial position?
10. What are the main differences between the front pages of each of the newspapers shown on page 29? Mention content, style, size.

Television and Radio

Television and radio are expected to fufil the same functions as newspapers with the exception of influence. Programmes should display balance, allowing the views of both sides to be heard on controversial subjects. Presentation should be impartial and news coverage accurate. As well as taking care not to offend against good taste, there are codes of guidance on violence in television programmes, especially during hours when large numbers of children are likely to be viewing. The Independent Broadcasting Authority (IBA) also operates a code of advertising standards and practice. Both the BBC and IBA answer to a Complaints Commission on issues such as unfair treatment or infringement of privacy, and similar complaints about programmes and programme content.

TELEVISION

What is entertaining to one person may not be to another. For example, a ballet programme on BBC2 may be preferred by some people to a sports programme on BBC1 or ITV. BBC1 and ITV concentrate on family entertainment and programmes of wide appeal, while BBC2 puts greater emphasis on experiment and on serious cultural and documentary programmes, together with programmes for minority tastes. In a similar way, Channel 4 caters for tastes and interests not covered by the ITV channel. It has to provide educational programmes, and give opportunities for independent producers to show programmes.

In 1983, both BBC and IBA began early morning television programmes. These provide a mixture of news, weather, and magazine elements, and have a huge potential audience. Starting some weeks earlier than its IBA counterpart, BBC's Breakfast Time has proved highly successful. ITV's TV-AM, set up as a profitmaking company, has found problems attracting advertisers (as did Channel 4) with its smaller audience, and has had to alter its format to gain viewers.

Both BBC and IBA have teletext systems (CEEFAX and ORACLE) which, on specially adapted television sets, allow viewers to choose a display of pages of written information on the screen. This system also allows subtitles to be shown with certain programmes.

Future developments, along the lines of American television, are Pay TV, which has had a short experimental trial, and Cable Television which aims to give more variety and choice for the viewer with the minimum of outside controls. This might mean Cable channels of pop music, news, adult movies, children's cartoons, quiz programmes.

Many people now own video recorders, which allow television programmes to be recorded and viewed at a more convenient time. Films can also be hired to be shown using the recorders and television set.

RADIO

BBC radio has four national stations, each attempting to provide a different service:

Radio 1 popular music
Radio 2 light music and sport
Radio 3 classical music, adult education and programmes of artistic and intellectual interest
Radio 4 UK news and information, with many speech programmes: drama, art, talks; school broadcasts

Letter to the *Glenforth Courier* – TV page

Sir – Last night on BBC1 there was a disgusting play with naked women and a lot of violence. Tonight's viewing has a film that was for over-eighteens in the cinema and a repeat of an American detective series. ITV is just the same. BBC2 has ballet and a programme about splitting the atom, and Channel 4 offers us an in-depth look at a surgical operation, or current affairs.

I don't pay my TV licence for this sort of thing. I want entertainment. I think ordinary viewers should stop paying their licences. That would make the TV companies change their ways.

Jane Briggs (Mrs)

Our TV Reporter writes:

First of all, you'd only hit the BBC by not paying a licence, Mrs Briggs, and you'd be breaking the law, too. The IBA gets its money from adverts, so every time you buy beans or perfume you pay indirectly for IBA programmes.

The companies just don't have enough cash to produce new programmes every night – so you get repeats – but a lot of people ask to see programmes again. America buys some of our best programmes and we take theirs: it gives a bit of variety. In our TV ratings item, you'll see some of the American series are very popular.

BBC2 is a special channel designed to cater for minority interests: with documentaries, Open University programmes and items of interest to special groups of people like rugby fans or opera enthusiasts, but it also has pop music and hobby programmes. Channel 4 does roughly the same thing for IBA.

The TV companies try very hard to keep family viewing hours free from 'adult' type plays and films (like the ones you are complaining about). They think most children will be in bed by the time they screen these – at the end of peak viewing time. If you feel very strongly about a programme you can write directly to the TV company's complaints department.

In 1984 there were 27 local radio stations run by the BBC as well as 37 independent or commercial stations. The BBC local radio stations take part of the national programmes from Radio 4. The commercial stations such as Radio Clyde and Capital Radio provide a wide service of local news and information, various kinds of music and other entertainment, consumer advice and phone-ins.

FINANCE

The BBC is financed by the sale of television licences: £15 for black and white and £46 for colour. In 1982 there were about $18\frac{1}{2}$ million licenced television sets in Britain, and of these, 14 million were colour sets. The BBC also receives grants from Parliament for external services, profits from BBC publications, including the *Radio Times,* and the export of television programmes.

Each of the IBA companies is financed by the sale of advertising time, the sale of programmes to other companies and the export of programmes. From this income they have to pay rental to the IBA for transmitting stations and a levy to the government which is related to profits.

Questions

1. What are the main differences between the programmes which appear on BBC1, BBC2, ITV and Channel 4?
2. In what ways do commercial, local and national radio stations compete with each other?
3. What can the public do to complain about anything they see or hear on television or radio?
4. What efforts can the BBC make to keep down licence fees?
5. What efforts can IBA programme companies make to ensure a profit for their shareholders?
6. Name as many of the other IBA TV companies as you can. What programmes, if any, does your ITV company take from them?

PART 2
The Economy

1. The Structure of a Mixed Economy

Industry

Industries in Britain can be grouped in various ways, depending on whether we are interested in who owns them; how they are organised; whether they are declining or expanding; or what they produce.

WHO OWNS INDUSTRY?

The firms in the country, which together make up the country's industries, can be owned and run by individuals or groups of people who keep any **profits** made (and suffer any losses). These people take whatever decisions are necessary on such questions as what, when, where and how to produce. This is sometimes known as 'free enterprise' economy. ICI and Fine Fare are examples of private enterprises.

Alternatively, industries, or firms, can be owned and run by the government on behalf of the public. Profits and losses are shared by the whole country and the answers to such questions as where and how to produce can take other issues into account, such as the best interests of the country. This is sometimes called 'State controlled' economy. The National Coal Board and British Rail are examples of public enterprises or nationalised industries.

Britain's economy is a 'mixed' economy. Some industries and some firms are owned privately (by shareholders) and some publicly (by government). Sometimes the government owns some or even most of the **shares** in a firm. Many companies operating in Britain are, in fact, owned by individuals from other countries, or even by the governments of other countries. Such companies, which operate in more than one country, are called **multinationals,** or trans-nationals. Examples are Exxon and Ford.

The government tries to improve performance in all these kinds of firms and industries, by giving advice and grants of money, and by the use of taxes and laws. Each government also tries to make sure that the British people receive the best possible standard of living. How this is to be done often leads to disagreements.

HOW IS INDUSTRY ORGANISED?

An industry may be very small – one or two people who work for themselves, termed 'self-employed' – for example, joiners, small shopkeepers; or it may be very large, often using mass-production techniques, in which workers specialise in their own tasks. Mass-production, based on **economies of scale,** is efficient but the work can be boring for the employees.

A company can also diversify, that is, it can produce many different kinds of products or **services,** so that if one fails or becomes less popular, others can be relied on to save the company from collapse. A company might even try to be involved in all aspects of the product from finding the raw materials, through producing the finished article, to selling it. This gives the company greater control over its own business.

DECLINE OR EXPANSION?

Some industries have become less important to the economy than they were, in that they employ fewer people, or produce fewer goods, or are less likely to make a profit. They are known as declining industries (e.g. shipbuilding and steel). Expanding industries are those which are presumed to have a secure future, with an increasing **demand** for their product (e.g. oil and electronics).

WHAT IS PRODUCED?

Industries can be divided into three types: primary industry produces raw materials which are either extracted from the ground or sea (e.g. mining) or grown in it (e.g. farming and forestry); secondary industry involves **manufacturing** raw material into something which can be sold to the consumer (e.g. clothing or cars); tertiary industry involves giving a service, (e.g. hairdressing, transport, banking, **insurance**, or tourism).

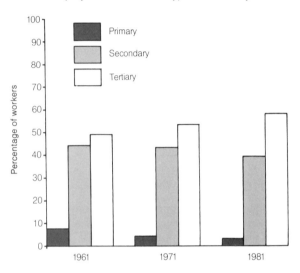

1 Employment in different types of industry

A CASE STUDY: Joe McPherson

Joe McPherson was a baker – a very good one – who sold loaves to a number of local shops. He thought he might make more money if he could bake more bread by taking on extra workers and getting some new electric ovens. To do this he needed money, but the bank wouldn't give him a big enough loan. His brother-in-law, Jimmy Cochrane, suggested that, if they joined their money together and formed a partnership, Joe could expand his business. Joe asked his mother to put some money in as well, and, though she agreed right away, Joe drew her a diagram of how the business worked (diagram 2).

The partnership worked: Joe had the extra money he needed and Jimmy was a skilled cake-maker. Part of the agreement was to change the name of the firm to 'McPherson and Cochrane'. Soon they were able to move to larger modern premises at a low rent on an industrial estate.

With the success of the partnership, Joe thought of expanding further by forming a private limited company. He would offer shares in the company to the rest of his family: if the firm failed they would lose only the amount they had invested; if it succeeded they could earn **interest** on their shares in two ways. His mother, who wanted to make sure of her income, bought stocks in the company. These gave her a fixed rate of interest, so that no matter what happened to the company's profits she would be guaranteed her income. Joe didn't think it showed much faith in the company! The rest of the family agreed to take ordinary shares which earned a dividend or income: usually the same every year, although in theory they could get more or less depending on the size of company profits.

With this extra investment, McPherson and Cochrane Ltd went from strength to strength. Their range of products widened: they began printing labels, wrapping paper and boxes for their cakes and bread ('**diversification**' Jimmy called it). He also thought it would be a good idea to move into grain farming and transport, so they would have control of earlier and later stages in the making and selling of bread. He gave this the grand title 'vertical **integration**'.

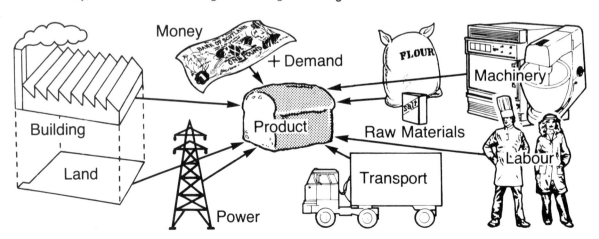

2 Necessary factors for production

Joe wasn't so happy about this. Where was the money for this extra **investment** to come from, since the family had no more? His bank manager suggested he make the company a public limited one and have shares sold on the Stock Exchange. This idea proved a success as many investors, including some pension funds, saw the potential in McPherson and Cochrane PLC.

As the bakeries expanded Joe had to bring in more machinery and 'production line' methods. This caused problems every now and then with some of Joe's employees. He sympathised with their complaint that standing beside a conveyor belt and doing the same task all day every day was boring. But since each worker was skilled in his or her own job it was difficult to vary their tasks. Sometimes there were shortages of wrapping paper because of transport difficulties, and if that happened, no bread was wrapped, and the workers had to be laid off. They certainly didn't like that, and it was bad for business too since less bread was sold. Joe eventually worked out a deal with the unions which improved things. Both sides were happy with the concessions made: the new staff canteens were particularly successful.

Joe discovered that the government and the EEC gave assistance to industries prepared to open factories in certain parts of the country with high unemployment (Assisted Areas). He got information about some of the **loans** and grants available, and was able to obtain a grant which enabled the business to expand further.

As the years went by, McPherson and Cochrane PLC became more and more of a success story. Joe, however, was not content to stick to the same methods of production. He saw that future success could only be certain if his company invested in more mechanisation. He brought in experts to research the most up-to-date ideas, and persuaded his directors to begin a massive investment programme. This involved the automation of many of the production processes, including the use of robots which replaced workers who had been performing repetitive and boring tasks. Many workers had to be persuaded to retire early or to take voluntary redundancy. Computers and microprocessors were also brought in to streamline many of the administrative procedures of the company, including payments of wages and stock control.

After fifteen years they had become a multinational company, with cakes and bread being made and sold throughout Europe. Almost every loaf of bread in Britain was made by McPherson and Cochrane. Competitors, apart from a few small businesses, had either been taken over or had given up. The Labour Government of the time began to

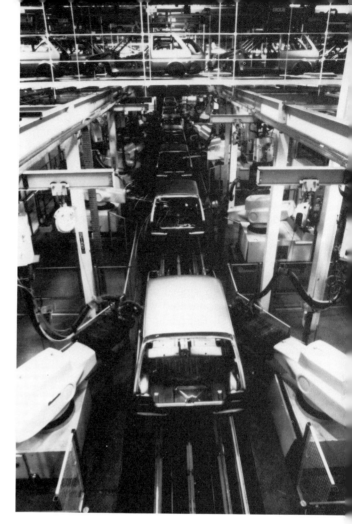

3 Robots on Metro assembly line

wonder if such an important industry as breadmaking should not be run and owned by the government on behalf of the nation. They thought it would allow them to plan the economy better, if steel, coal and bread were government-run. They believed that if these industries were nationalised, like electricity and gas, they would be more efficient because wasteful competition would be removed and more research and development could be carried out than individual companies such as Joe's were able to do. Joe was horrified at such interference. He wrote a very strong letter to the government saying that he was in favour of free enterprise, since nationalisation always meant more **bureaucracy** and paperwork; that nationalised industries were impersonal businesses which caused consumer dissatisfaction and laziness in workers; that people wouldn't be able to choose which bread to buy as there would be no competition and that the taxpayer would have to stump up, first to buy and then to subsidise the business. It was unfair that an Act of Parliament could remove his business from him and appoint a new board of directors, responsible not to him and his shareholders, but a minister of the government and Parliament. After all, he had built it up from nothing.

After a General Election, a Conservative government took over. Joe knew there was no more fear of nationalisation of his business. In fact, he agreed with their policy of privatisation. The new government wanted to sell as much of the public sector to private individuals as possible. It would not only raise money for the government and so allow them to keep taxation down, but it was also a good idea to have the government running only the firms and industries which no one else could run. This would free many others to compete in the private sector. Joe was so much in favour of this idea that for the first time in his business life he put money into something not connected with bread. He bought shares in British Petroleum and British Telecom, because he was sure they were a good investment and would make more money for him.

Joe planned to use the profits from these shares and from his shares in McPherson and Cochrane to provide income for his retirement. He was thinking of handing over full control to his board of directors, and he had high hopes that his son, Joe Junior, would become the new chairman.

Questions

1. What is meant by a mixed economy?
2. Look at Fig. 1. Which type of industry is growing? Which type of industry has the smallest workforce?
3. Look at Fig. 2. List the factors needed to produce something, and give an example of each.
4. In what four ways did Joe get extra money for his business?
5. If Joe had owned a men's clothing shop, what could he have done to (a) diversify, (b) integrate vertically?
6. What two things caused trouble between Joe and his workers? How did he improve things?
7. What help was the government prepared to offer Joe? Why?
8. What are the arguments for and against nationalisation?
9. What are the arguments for and against privatisation?

The Government and Industry

Governments, of whatever political party, try to involve themselves in the British economy. If industries are efficient and are taking advantage of opportunities to do well, then the whole economy of the country is more likely to improve. Governments are blamed if there are unsolved economic problems such as unemployment and **inflation**; if people do not feel they are better off than they used to be; and if other problems such as effective defence, poverty and unfairness in society are not dealt with. All of these problems can be more effectively dealt with if the government encourages and helps industries to succeed.

There are a wide variety of measures which a government can take to improve industrial performance.

NATIONALISED INDUSTRIES

If the government feels that an industry is very important to the nation, then it can take the industry under State control to be run by a board appointed

4 Largest industrial organisations ranked by turnover

Private sector	£million	Public sector	£million
British Petroleum	30624	Electricity council and boards	8471
Shell Transport/trading	18782	BNOC	5752
BAT Trading	9265	British Telecom	5708
ICI	6581	British Gas Corp.	5235
Esso	5324	National Coal Board	4728
Shell UK	5182	British Steel Corp.	3443
Unilever	4935		
Imperial Group	4526		
General Electric Co.	3462		
Grand Metropolitan	3221		
Czarnikow Group	3123		
Ford Motor Co.	3073		

Britain Handbook 1983 (adapted)

by the government **minister** concerned. A Labour Government made this decision about the coal industry in 1947, because **nationalisation** seemed the only way to modernise such an important basic industry. The railways were nationalised at the same time. They were seen to be an essential service where wasteful competition should be avoided. Nationalisation would also mean that a more complete service could be provided. Many routes, (for example, those in remote areas) would always make a loss, and few private companies would be prepared to run these services.

Every year a House of Commons Select Committee looks at the accounts and reports of each nationalised industry. Some nationalised industries run at a loss year after year (although they may be providing a service to the rest of the economy), and the government has to find the money, out of taxation, to cover these losses. The government could tell the industry to stop making losses, and to 'break even', or make a profit. This might mean cutting back on the services provided, or finding other ways to save money: redundancies through closing parts of the industry; increased prices; bringing in 'trouble shooters' to find out where things are going wrong. Most nationalised industries try to 'break even' over the years.

Industries and firms which are controlled by the government can lead the way in controlling wages and prices. A price rise in one of the nationalised industries might mean user industries having to put up their prices, and other industries following the lead and putting up their own prices. However, if nationalised industries hold prices down and keep wage increases low, other industries have an example to follow.

Recent Conservative governments have felt that some nationalised industries, or parts of them, should be returned to the private sector. Having to compete with other firms would make them more efficient and having to answer to profit-conscious shareholders would make them more aware of costs.

FIRMS PARTLY OR WHOLLY OWNED BY GOVERNMENT

There are many firms in which the government owns all or some of the shares. A number of these were bought when the National Enterprise Board (a government body) was involved in giving money to or buying shares in firms facing short-term problems. This was sometimes called 'backdoor nationalisation'. With ownership of shares in companies such as British Leyland, British Petroleum, British National Oil Corporation (BNOC), British

Aerospace, National Freight Consortium, the government not only has a big say in the plans of these companies, it can also raise money when necessary by selling some shares in a company. Between 1979 and 1983, for example, the Conservative Government raised £2 billion by selling some of its shares. It planned to raise more by selling off profitable parts of British Telecom and British Airways. This action fits in with the Conservative Government's policy of privatisation.

ASSISTED AREAS

The government operates a scheme to encourage investors and companies to set up or expand businesses in selected areas of Britain. This is intended to strengthen the national economy and provide secure jobs. Many of the measures on offer are deliberately biased in favour of certain areas of the country as the map (Fig. **6**) shows. Some apply to any area of Britain if they improve the competitiveness of industry.

Regional Development **Grants,** to help build a factory, or buy machinery, are given automatically in a Special Development Area (22% grant) or a Development Area (15% grant). This means that, if the investor puts in most of the money, the govern-

5 Industrial advert

ment will pay the rest. Selective Regional Assistance can also be given where a project would create more jobs or save existing ones but cannot go ahead without help. The Department of Trade and Industry will support innovation (the introduction of new processes) by providing grants for research and development.

Other forms of help are available in Assisted Areas. Factories built by local **authorities,** New Towns, the Scottish Development Agency and other Development Agencies or the Highlands and Islands Development Board are available for a rent-free period or for sale; small businesses can get loans quickly. Workers' Co-operatives, owned and controlled by the people who work in them, can be set up and given advice by government agencies.

The European Regional Development Fund, a branch of the European Community (EEC), allocates money each year (a quota to each member country) and helps pay for schemes including those which provide the **infrastructure** for industry (roads, water and sewage).

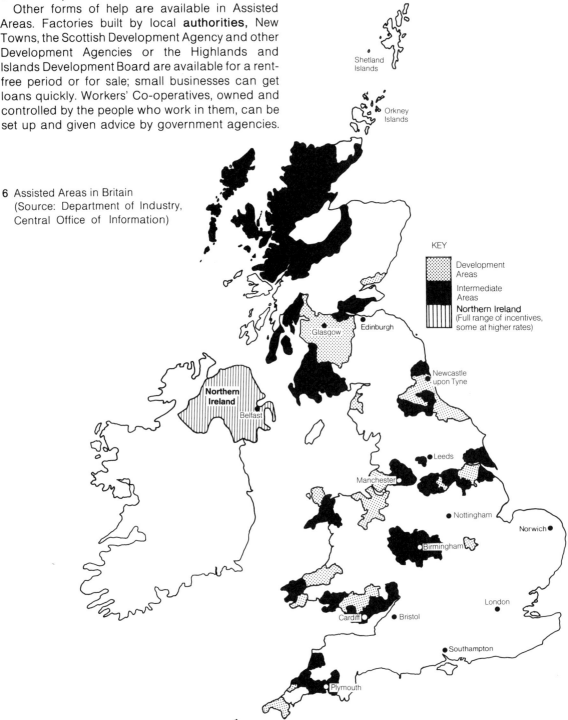

6 Assisted Areas in Britain
(Source: Department of Industry, Central Office of Information)

KEY

Development Areas

Intermediate Areas

Northern Ireland
(Full range of incentives, some at higher rates)

Areas particularly badly hit by the economic recession can be given the special status of an Enterprise Zone. These are small areas which need massive amounts of help even to offset the worst aspects of unemployment and industrial decline. Areas such as Belfast, Clydebank, Newcastle and Corby, for example, get the same assistance as a Special Development Area, plus exemption from rates on property and from some other taxes, further loans and help with simplified planning procedure. A firm might therefore feel encouraged to take advantage of these various offers and set up business in these areas rather than elsewhere. This benefits both the firm itself and an area desperately in need of employment.

DEVELOPMENT AGENCIES AND CORPORATIONS

Development Agencies and Corporations were set up in the mid 1970s to spearhead the revival of industry. They have wide powers including the building of factories, clearing land for industrial use, giving loans to and investing in private companies. Many business premises and leisure areas which have replaced areas of urban decay around the country, to some extent, owe their existence to these agencies.

For example, by 1983, the Scottish Development Agency was financially involved in 725 Scottish businesses. Projects included the promotion of technology, the construction of industrial buildings and offices, help to small businesses, land renewal and environmental projects to replace unsightly derelict land.

To some extent these agencies and corporations are in competition with one another for the same potential business ventures. Areas which are not covered in this way often feel they are being **discriminated** against in the search for new businesses.

OTHER GOVERNMENT MEASURES TO IMPROVE INDUSTRIAL PERFORMANCE

These include the following.
● *Changing levels of taxation.* Direct taxes (income tax) or indirect taxes (such as VAT) can be changed to allow the buying public more or less money to spend.
● *Altering the ease or difficulty of getting credit.* Interest rates can be raised or lowered to make borrowing more or less expensive. Restrictions on the size of the loan or the deposit needed can also be changed.

● *Changing laws about conditions of work, early retirement, mergers and monopolies.*
● *Raising or lowering public spending.* If more money is allocated to education, for example, this can mean more business for book publishers. But if local authorities are told to cut their spending, this can affect employment in the area and the quality of infrastructure designed to help industry, including roads, public transport and education.
● *Controlling inflation.* Knowing prices are unlikely to rise above a given level might encourage a firm to invest, and perhaps modernise its workplace. But workers in the firm might be unhappy that their claim for higher wages is affected by government guidelines on wages which aim to keep inflation down.

Questions

1. Why does government get involved in the British economy?
2. If an industry is nationalised, what control does the government have over its operation?
3. What assistance is given to companies who set up in an Assisted Area?
4. What might the views of each of the following be on an area given special status? Potential investors; firms already in the area; unemployed in the area; unemployed in another area.

2. British Industries

When the latest world recession began in the early 1970s, Britain's industrial base was already established. It consisted mainly of textiles and heavy industries such as shipbuilding, steel and engineering which had very large workforces. Most of these industries had come to rely on imported raw materials, and sold the finished articles abroad. This made it harder for Britain than almost any other developed country to adapt quickly to the changes which were needed to meet the challenges and hardships of the recession. Raw materials had become more expensive, and traditional markets abroad had started to buy goods produced in other countries instead of Britain, claiming that the British goods were too expensive or too poor a quality to compete effectively. Firms and companies which have kept going have often been unable to invest in the new machinery and technology required to compete with firms from other countries.

In the short term, most of the traditional industries have declined, with thousands of firms and branch factories going **bankrupt,** closing down or cutting back. Millions of workers (and potential workers) have become unemployed and parts of Britain have earned the reputation of being industrial wastelands with severe **economic** and **social** problems.

Some industries have survived the bad times by adapting quickly to the need for change, streamlining their production with investment in new working methods and cutting back their workforce. Salespeople have gone out and fought hard to win orders for their products against tough competition. New products have been developed to replace those no longer required. For example, many shipyards were re-equipped to make oil rigs to meet the demands of the North Seal oil industry. (Now, however, many of these yards are having to think again as demand for oil rigs in turn declines.) New markets have been found for traditional goods, in Third World countries and in the home market. Some people have moved away from areas suffering most from industrial decline, setting up home again in areas with greater prospects of employment. New industries have been firmly established in this country, taking advantage of the incentives offered not only by the government but by the demands for new products, such as computer technology, electronics, and **services** such as tourism.

One way to understand the changes taking place in British industry is to take a look at one industry from six of the major groups of industries in Britain: the declining sector (steel); the expanding sector (electronics); energy creation (coal and oil); transport (rail); manufacturing (cars); and the service sector (tourism).

Steel

Steel is a basic material from which many other products are made in the areas of transport, building, machinery, consumer goods and engineering. The steel industry is therefore affected by what happens to the demand for these products.

In 1967, the steel industry was nationalised (for the second time) and the British Steel Corporation (BSC) was created to manage the fourteen companies. 85% of Britain's crude steel is produced by BSC. The private sector of the industry is mainly involved in finished products.

An enormous amount of investment in new production methods (replacing open-hearth steelmaking with the basic oxygen process and the electric arc process) came in the early 1970s. Unfortunately this was followed by a world-wide recession which left the industry increasing its capacity to make steel at a time when demand was falling, both at home and abroad. Foreign competition from old rivals such as the United States and Europe and from new steel makers in Brazil, India

7 Employment in selected industries, Great Britain (thousands)

	1961	1971	1982
Agriculture, forestry fishing	692	421	326
Coal	663	346	260
Petroleum and gas	3	2	26
Oil refining	28	23	14
Iron and steel	316	269	122
Electronics			
Radio and electronic components	93	128	106
Electronic computers	-	43	59
Radio, radar, electronic capital goods	-	95	107
Motor vehicle	408	502	304
Railways	410	240	192
Hotels	232	219	272
Restaurants and cafés	150	151	188

(Source: *Annual Abstract of Statistics*)

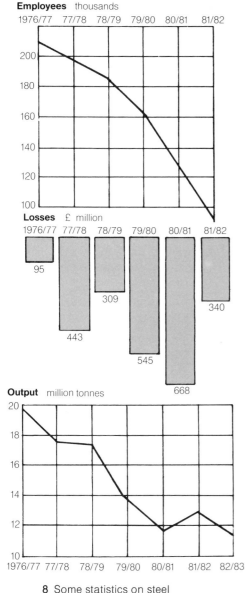

8 Some statistics on steel
(Source: *The Times*, 9 June 1982)

The effects of these solutions have been severe. The industry still does not make a profit, even after the drastic reduction in capacity and workforce. And the 'social cost' hardship to families and communities has been incalculable. The fall in demand for steel has been caused by the fall in demand for products made from steel. When a major buyer such as a shipyard or a car plant closes, this increases the pressure on BSC to close another steel mill. Even if it is a modern plant with high productivity, if no one wants what it makes, it either stays open at much less than full capacity, **subsidised** by the government, or it closes. When it closes, it takes with it many other jobs in the area, since it is usually a major employer. A nearby coal pit may close; less freight is carried on the local railway line; nearby shops close since there is less money in the area.

Electronics

The electronics industry is almost entirely within the private sector. A high proportion of the firms established are branch factories in Britain of American and Japanese companies. They have been attracted to Britain to take advantage of the European markets. Government and its agencies specifically encourage high technology industries to set up in this country, pointing out the advantages of grants and other incentives as well as the reputation of the workforces already employed. As a result, for example, parts of Central Scotland have been nicknamed 'Silicon Glen' (after 'Silicon Valley' in California) because of the high proportion of factories involved in production based on the silicon chip. Care has been taken to make sure that the full range of the industry exists in Britain, from hardware components to software and research and development.

A dramatic change is taking place in all areas of our lives, because of the use of micro-processors. Integrated circuits can be placed on a flat piece of silicon, as a tiny 'chip', and can be made quickly and very cheaply. These are used in the manufacture of radar and navigation aids, telecommunications, consumer goods such as calculators, watches, video equipment and computers. This industry, in turn, services other industries, providing, for example, automated production methods such as robots. This, inevitably, means a reduction in the need for workers, unless the industry itself expands.

Though electronics has been regarded as a fast-growing industry, and has often been presented as

and Korea, left BSC in a weak position. This was worsened by soaring costs and cut-throat prices. The workforce was reputed to be larger than necessary and to have a poor productivity record. All this made profit unlikely, even in the long term.

The solutions have been drastic. The workforce has been cut by more than half, with widespread redundancies. Steelmills, judged to be either old fashioned or surplus to present requirements, have been closed. Sales of British steel have been agressively sought in the domestic and export markets. The government has been asked to wait a bit longer for a profit-making industry.

9 Machine operators in a computer factory

Energy

The production of energy is a vital part of the nation's economy. It enables industry to operate and has countless uses for **consumers**. Primary sources of energy in Britain are coal, natural gas, petroleum and nuclear power. These are often used to turn energy into its secondary state, electricity. All of these industries, apart from the production of oil and gas and the refining of oil, are publicly owned. This makes the government, and the Secretary of State for Energy in particular, responsible for ensuring a reliable, plentiful and safe supply for all users. Most forms of energy come from finite resources which will eventually run out altogether, so it is important to discourage wasteful consumption. This can be done partly by encouraging consumers to save energy and partly by a policy of pricing energy highly so that consumers cannot afford to waste it.

a success story for other industries to follow, it has not been without problems, both within the industry and in society at large. It is accepted that too little British investment has gone into the industry. Thus profits made have not benefited Britain. Moreover, past experience in other industries has shown that, in times of recession, the branch factories owned by foreign companies are likely to close first. A high proportion of the workforce is female, and this has helped to change the traditional role of the male as wage earner.

Employment in the industry is split between the highly skilled technical staff and the relatively non-skilled assembly workers. Many processes of manufacture in the industry are themselves being done by automated methods. Finally, in a rapidly changing technology, some factories will have a limited lifespan before they themselves become out of date, and close. There have been some signs that the boom may be over. The total number of workers in the industry has fallen over the last six years.

The effect of the industry on the economy and society has been revolutionary. But some workers, for example those in newspaper production, have resisted the introduction of new technology, feeling that their jobs are threatened. There is certainly no doubt that our lives are being changed and some people feel the change is happening too quickly. National unemployment is rising as a result of this new technology. The improvement in our lifestyle may not be enough to compensate for this.

10 Energy consumption in Britain in 1971 and 1981

(a) **1971**

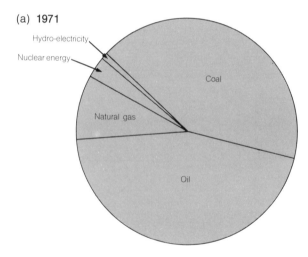

(b) **1981**

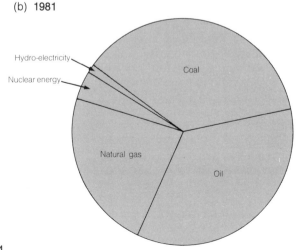

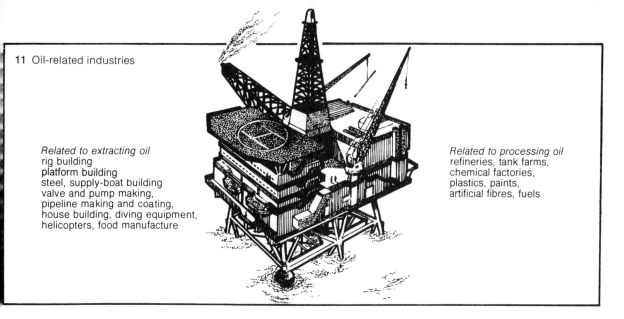

11 Oil-related industries

Related to extracting oil
rig building
platform building
steel, supply-boat building
valve and pump making,
pipeline making and coating,
house building, diving equipment,
helicopters, food manufacture

Related to processing oil
refineries, tank farms,
chemical factories,
plastics, paints,
artificial fibres, fuels

NORTH SEA OIL

The first discovery of oil in the British sector of the North Sea was made in 1969, in the Forties Field. In 1975, the first oil was brought ashore, by tanker from the Argyll Field. Since then, licences to explore for oil in the North Sea have been issued to private oil companies. The British National Oil Corporation, set up in 1975, helps to control exploration, development, pipeline installation and refining and to control the rate of depletion of the oil to ensure the greatest long-term benefit to Britain. In 1982, the oil production part of BNOC became Britoil and the intention is to sell this off to the private sector.

The discovery of oil in the North Sea has made, and will continue to make, a great difference to the British economy. The boost given to oil-related industries, for example, has kept unemployment lower than it might otherwise have been.

Britain's Balance of Payments has also benefited. In the past, Britain had to import large amounts of crude oil amounting to about 18% of the total imports bill. This oil came from the Middle East, Algeria, Nigeria and Venezuela, and is no longer needed in such large quantities. Some oil still has to be imported, as North Seal oil is mainly light oil and

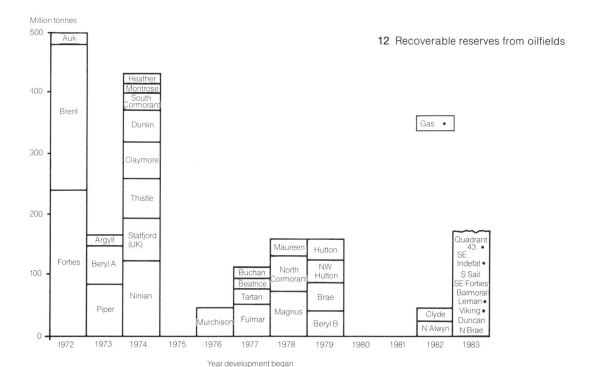

12 Recoverable reserves from oilfields

has to be mixed with heavier imported oils. But Britain produces more than enough oil for its own needs. By 1983, Britain was the world's fifth largest producer of oil; almost half the oil it produced was exported.

Governments have been concerned that the British people should benefit directly from the oil in the North Sea. Revenue has been raised from the oil companies by the usual tax on profits and from a Petroleum Revenue Tax. When there were signs that this tax was turning oil companies away from exploring for new oil fields, it was lowered to encourage further exploration and investment.

The industry has had its critics. They mention the effect on the North East of Scotland, where people's lifestyles have been changed by the influx of oil workers on the oil rigs and related services. Accidents and deaths of workers serving the industry might in some cases have been avoided if more research had gone into the stresses on materials used in the harsh conditions of the North Sea. More advantage might have been taken of the discovery of oil, perhaps by giving the multi-national oil companies less control and attempting to channel the benefits of the discovery back to the British people. The oil is going to run out in the future, but that date could have been postponed if it had been extracted more slowly and not exported. Despite these criticisms, there are thousands of people who owe their jobs to the discovery of North Sea oil, and society has benefited from the **revenue** raised.

COAL

Coal is one of the foundations on which Britain's industrial revolution was based, and is still an important raw material and source of power.

The Labour Government of 1945–51 considered that coal was so important to Britain that the industry should be nationalised, so in 1947 it was put under the management of the National Coal Board, which is responsible to the Minister for Energy and to Parliament.

Since the 1950s there has been a fall in demand for coal, mainly due to changing tastes, the creation of smokeless zones, the abandonment of steam power on the railways, the discovery of natural gas to replace coal gas, and competition from other fuels, especially oil. Many pits have been closed because they are not making a profit, and advanced mining machines, self-advancing powered roof supports and improved underground transport have led to a further reduction in employment.

The future of the coal industry is not entirely certain. Although coal will still be required, alterna-

13 Arthur Scargill meets the new Chairman of the National Coal Board, Ian MacGregor, September 1983

tive sources of energy are more attractive to the government and most consumers. There is disagreement over what to do about pits in which it costs more to produce the coal than can be made from selling it. The government thinks these uneconomic pits should be closed and the miners made redundant. Coal workers, however, argue that, if coal is a valuable resource, it should be mined regardless (within reason) of cost. The policy of closures has so far meant a reduction in the number of pits from 700 in 1960 to under 200 in 1983, and of miners from 600 000 to under 200 000. Miners may be reluctant to allow the industry to shrink further, while the government is concerned to ensure efficiency through new technology and higher productivity.

Railways

British Rail is a nationalised industry, run by the British Railways Board but owned by the government on behalf of the public. It provides an important service both to customers and to the economy by carrying passengers and freight (bulky heavy material such as coal, steel). Its Inter-City services and local stopping and commuter services around major cities carry hundreds of millions of passengers a year.

For many years, however, the railways have been of concern to governments, mainly because they have not made a profit and needed a subsidy from the government. They have been criticised for inefficiency, for requiring government money (though less than most European railways), and for sometimes providing a poor service for passengers. A review of the railways, the Serpell Report, published in 1983, claimed that British Rail did not provide good value for money. On the other hand, there have been enormous changes in recent years in the development of a more modern railway system. Steam trains have been replaced, first by diesel and then electric trains. Indeed the British Railways Board thinks further electrification is vital to British Rail's future. Tracks and signalling have been improved to meet the new faster running speeds. Computers are used to monitor the use made of rolling stock and some mechanisation of freight carrying has increased efficiency and streamlined the service.

British Rail is faced with the following problems.
1. *Fares.* British Rail often operates as a non-profit-making service. Many commuters would not use trains if a realistic fare was charged and remote and rural areas would become more isolated if lines were closed just because they lost money. It may not be possible to provide a good service and make a profit, so agreement would have to be reached with the government that a profit need not be made in all aspects of British Rail's service.
2. *Equipment.* Maintenance and routine replacement of equipment has fallen behind over the years and much of the rolling stock is in desperate need of replacement. This is putting a strain on the service. Money could be saved but only at the expense of lowering safety standards; basically more money is needed to modernise.
3. *Workforce.* Wages make up a large part of the total cost of running British Rail. The workforce has been reluctant to agree to some of the changes which are thought necessary to increase productivity and efficiency. Nevertheless, the number of workers was reduced from 410 000 in 1961 to only

15 Passenger transport in Great Britain (thousand million passenger kilometres)		
	1971	*1981*
Total	423.4	502.3
Air	2.0	2.6
Rail	35.4	34.9
Road (public service)	51.0	38.0
Road (private cars)	330.0	422.0
Bicycle	5.0	4.8

192 000 in 1982. Workers have shown that they are willing to change their work practices if they are given compensation and if they see the changes as necessary.
4. *Competition.* Lorries have the advantage over rail freight of providing door-to-door service. Motorway express buses and airlines are recent competitors for long-distance passenger transport. For ordinary travel, cars are more convenient and private. Advertising, special offers and reduced fares for off-peak travel have attracted extra passengers to the railways, but more money needs to be spent to promote the service effectively.
5. *Recession.* The railways, as a key part of the transport industry, have been badly hit by the recession. Higher unemployment means fewer goods are being carried by train. This in turn reduces revenue and any possibility of making a profit.
6. *Investment.* The Board faces a dilemma. They are expected to provide a service at low cost, yet they cannot provide an efficient up-to-date service without spending vast amounts of money. The Serpell Report offered a selection of strategies for the government to choose from. They ranged from keeping the existing 10 400 route miles open and making huge losses, to reducing to a minimum core of 1600 route miles and making a small profit. The choice remains to be made.

14 Electric train

The Car Industry

For many years, the production of motor cars has been a major manufacturing industry in Britain. Today, this production is concentrated in the hands of four main companies. British Leyland (BL), a merger of many previously separate companies, has a majority public shareholding. The other three companies could all be considered multi-nationals, owned by companies abroad. They are Ford (American), Vauxhall (American) and Talbot (French).

Each company produces parts for, and assembles, cars both for the home market and for export. A wide range of cars is required, to cater for all tastes, from the small car, through the family saloon, to the large luxury car. The car industry used to be a big Balance of Payments earner, until the mid-1970s, when imports began to outstrip exports. However, the car industry is still the largest manufacturing exporter and the largest earner of foreign currency. It therefore attracts much interest and support from the government.

This industry depends on as many as 400 component parts, made in smaller factories. The parts are assembled by a skilled engineering workforce on a conveyor belt system of assembly-line work. This is a production method designed to achieve **economies of scale**, but the work is often found to be repetitive and tedious, and can be disrupted if parts are not delivered on time for any reason.

Some of the major problems in the industry have been the following.

1. *Competition from imports.* Many people prefer a foreign-made car, but every foreign car sold means one fewer British car is required. If it were not for the loyalty of other British companies buying British cars for company use (e.g. fleet cars) and for an unofficial quota restriction on Japanese imports, the problem would be even greater. In addition, many 'British' cars contain foreign-made parts and are merely assembled in Britain.

2. *Competition between the four major producers in Britain.* The British new car market has been described as a jungle. There is a constant struggle to sell all types of new cars to the various potential customers: small fuel-saving cars, family cars, executive and prestige cars, company and sales representatives' cars, cars for car hire companies. In the battle to sell, companies have to make special offers and try to underprice each other, until the profit margin becomes very low indeed.

3. *The priorities of the companies.* During bad times, the British-owned company (BL) is under greater pressure than the others to keep its factories open rather than close down and make workers redundant. In the past, multi-nationals have closed down branch factories in Britain and taken the machinery elsewhere in Europe. Government concern for BL has led to massive subsidies, while the other three companies have been propped up by their parent company.

4. *The reputation of the British car industry.* Industrial relations disputes have given the industry a largely undeserved though damaging reputation. Coupled with accusations of poor quality, unreliable delivery dates and poor after-sales service, this has often led customers to buy elsewhere.

5. *The effect of the world economy.* As a major manufacturing industry, the car industry is quickly and severely hit by any recession. Demand for cars declines, and this in turn affects the demand for all the parts and materials used in the car industry, from steel to components. As a result of the present recession, there is great over-capacity in car manufacturing. This has led to widespread redundancies and factory closures as the industry adapts to meet the needs of the 1980s.

A big effort is being made to sell British cars rather than lose out to foreign competitors. Investment in high-technology robots to make the cars, and computers to ensure they are reliable, will help, if the finance is available. New ranges of cars are being introduced to attract customers and avoid dependence on one model. Productivity is being improved, as part of an efficiency drive (in 1979 BL produced 5.9 cars per worker, whereas in 1983 it produced 14.2 cars per worker; but in Japan production is 19 cars per worker). Costs have to be cut, particularly by reducing the workforce and cutting factory space.

The attempt to bring the British car industry into line with its competitors has had harsh consequences for thousands of workers, their families and communities. A manufacturing industry has had to learn to change and adapt.

Tourism

The Tourist industry is made up of a wide variety of kinds of employment: mainly in hotels, restaurants, shops, sports and leisure facilities, but also indirectly in other services supplying these. One and a half million people are currently employed directly or indirectly in the industry, which is growing all the time. It is of considerable value to the British economy as a major employer and earner of foreign exchange.

Almost all the industry is privately owned, from hotels and other accommodation, to shops and entertainment. The travel enterprises are a mixture of private (e.g. coaches) and public (e.g. rail). The British Tourist Authority, together with Tourist Boards for Scotland, England and Wales and local tourist bodies, usually receive government funds to help with publicity campaigns, advice, information and advertising. This is designed to encourage people, both foreigners and British, to make use of the tourist **facilities** available in this country.

It is important to make the resources in Britain act as a magnet for tourists so that foreign currency can be earned and British money spent in this country rather than abroad. A strong pound and high rate of inflation can discourage foreign tourists, as can the traditional British weather. However, the tourist industry is able to concentrate on selling types of holidays which do not rely on hot weather for their success. These include many of the following 'British' attractions: history and cultural heritage; beautiful scenery; London and the Royal Family. Some foreign tourists (e.g. Americans) are attracted to Britain because English is spoken. Newer attractions are also being developed, such as conference facilities for business people, trade fair and exhibition facilities; self-catering accommodation and camping and caravanning. This in turn can stimulate investment in transport, hotels, sports centres and the arts, which can benefit local people too.

By encouraging people to bring money into Britain and discouraging many British holiday-makers from spending theirs abroad, the tourist industry has been one of the success stories of the 1980s.

Questions

1. What changes have industries had to make to cope with the recession?
2. Write a short summary for each of the industries under the following headings: ownership; main product; output or services; recent developments; problems and solutions.

16 A poster advertising a British holiday

3. Problems of the Economy

Introduction: Growth

The government of every country wants its economy to grow, bringing greater wealth and a higher standard of living to its citizens. Improvement in these is measured by calculating the gross national product (GNP): the total value of all that is produced by the country concerned.

The aim is not simply to have a high rate of economic growth, however. Experience has shown that when there is a period of fast growth (a boom) it tends to be followed by a period of stagnation (a slump) during which there is either no rise in the standard of living or an increase which is based on borrowed or printed money, neither of which is desirable. Since these booms and slumps lead to uncertainty for the future, governments aim for a steady annual growth rate.

A high and steady growth in the economy can be prevented by the following factors.

- *Inflation.* Rising prices may reduce demand for goods and also make them too expensive to sell abroad.
- *Balance of Payments.* A deficit, when we pay out more for foreign goods and services than we get from abroad for ours, means that our exports are struggling to compete abroad and that imports are being preferred to home-produced goods.
- *Unemployment.* If people with money to invest are unsure about the future, or prefer to invest elsewhere, then there will be no money for new enterprises and production methods to replace the older ones which proved unsuccessful against competitors.
- *Productivity.* If it takes our industry more working hours to produce the same quantity of goods as our competitors, then growth will be more difficult to achieve.

Before 1973, output from British industry was rising by about 3% a year. Following the huge increase in oil prices, however, the industrialised world went into a slump bringing about a world **recession**. British industry was particularly badly hit by this recession. Output fell more; unemployment **grew faster**; North Sea oil sales hid what would otherwise have been enormous Balance of Payments deficits, as British industries failed to compete in both the home and foreign markets. Industries **declined** and factories closed. The steel industry, the car industry and countless other industries are all producing a fraction of their former output.

The government of the day cannot be entirely blamed for the recession, any more than it could take all the credit for a recovery out of the trough. Britain is part of the world economy and is affected by what happens elsewhere. But there are steps which a government can take to offset the worst effects of an economic recession on individuals and try to make sure that British industry is ready to take full advantage when the upturn comes in the economy.

THE BUDGET

It is accepted that some things are best organised by a central **administration,** the government, rather than by individuals or small groups. To organise such services as defence, education and the Welfare State, money has to be raised from a variety of sources. The government therefore has to prepare a spending plan, or Budget, to try to balance the country's spending with its income. As with a family budget, if a balance is not achieved and the nation spends more than it gets in income, the country will be 'in the red' (deficit). If the government balances its Budget, or is 'in the black', then the nation has a better chance of prospering, though some people may suffer from the harsh measures needed to achieve this.

Traditionally the government introduces its Budget around April each year, although mini-budgets and other changes can be made as required. A Budget is normally a statement of the government's policy on money and taxation (monetary and fiscal policy). Basically it is concerned with income (revenue) and expenditure. Therefore, a Budget will give details of changes in taxation (direct and indirect), National Insurance contributions (both employers and employees), and the programme of government spending within each of the ministries. Each Budget should have an overall economic and financial plan.

There is also a social side to the Budget. A Chancellor of the Exchequer can allocate more money to any group in society, such as old-age pensioners or the unemployed. He or she can announce measures designed to lessen unemployment or inflation; and can even discourage smoking, drinking or gambling by increasing tax or duty on them.

17 (a) Public expenditure 1983–4

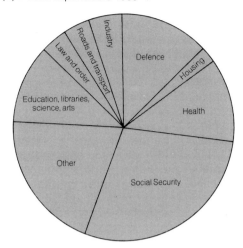

(b) Government income 1983–4

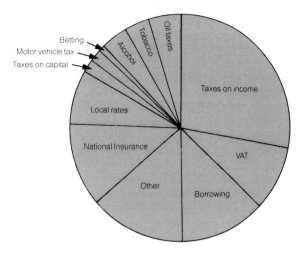

The Chancellor of the Exchequer will be attempting, in a Budget, to meet the needs of society (e.g. by increasing the retirement pension) and the economy (e.g. with measures to encourage investment). The success of the government and the Treasury in taking the correct steps not only improves Britain's economic prospects, but also helps to ensure the popularity of the government.

Three major economic problems have been a feature of economic and political life in Britain: unemployment, inflation and the Balance of Payments. All can have serious effects on individuals as well as the economy as a whole. Finding solutions is not simple since what might solve one economic problem for a short time might make another worse.

Questions

1. Why does a government want its country's economy to grow?
2. How is an economy's growth measured?
3. What is happening to an economy if it is described as having booms and slumps?
4. What is the Chancellor of the Exchequer trying to do when preparing the Budget?

Unemployment

To most people the word 'unemployed' simply means being out of work. Each month, the Department of Employment issues figures to show the level of unemployment in Britain. In 1982, the method of calculating the numbers of unemployed was changed to include only those who were claiming Unemployment Benefit. Some experts argue that there are many hundreds of thousands of other people who are unemployed but do not appear in the statistics, such as those near retiral age, former self-employed, and women who would work if there were jobs available.

The higher the unemployment figures are, the more concerned the public and the government become. It is accepted that it is impossible to achieve employment for everyone who is able to work, because there are always some people who are changing jobs and are temporarily unemployed, and some who, for one reason or another, do not want to find work (for example, those who are happy to stay at home while their partner goes out to work; some mothers of young children; some rich people; lazy people). Some people are unemployable, of course: for example, school children, the old and the severely mentally or physically handicapped. These groups are not usually included in the figures of unemployment.

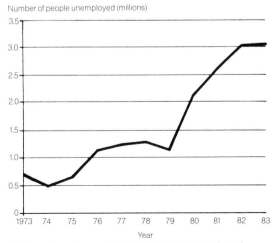

18 Number of people registered as unemployed

Scotland
15.1%

Northern Ireland
21.5%

North
17.3%

Yorkshire &
Humberside
14.0%

North West
15.7%

West
Midlands
11.9%

East
Midlands
15.1%

Wales
16.1%

East
Anglia
10.6%

Greater London
9.9%

South East
9.6%

South West
11.5%

THE EFFECTS OF UNEMPLOYMENT

● Unemployment means that one of the country's most important resources (labour) is not being fully used. This is as inefficient as not using all available farmland, or not mining all available coal in a mine.

● Unemployment means that some people are not helping to create things which could be sold and would put more money into the economy. People in work have a higher **standard of living** and can therefore buy more goods and services, which in turn means more jobs for more people.

● The loss of dignity involved in being unem-

ployed, especially in the long term, is harmful to individuals and their families.

● Unemployment Benefits and other sums of money paid to the unemployed and their families have to be met from government revenue.

● It has been suggested that there is a link between crime and high levels of unemployment, particularly among the young.

CAUSES OF UNEMPLOYMENT

Some people are out of work only temporarily: because they have left one job to look for another; or because their jobs are seasonal, and they are only in work for part of the year. Seasonal unemployment happens if workers are dependent on good weather (e.g. in the building industry) or if the demand for their services is high at certain times of year only (e.g. in tourism). However, most unemployed people have failed to find work for one of three reasons, none of which is really within their control. Firstly, many jobs have been taken over by new technology such as machinery, automation, or computers. This means that the same work can be done with fewer workers. Secondly, many skilled workers are no longer required because there has been a change in the structure of the economy and certain goods are not in demand. This may be because foreign imported goods have become more popular, fashions have changed or consumers choose to spend their money on something different. Thirdly, jobs have been lost because of a slump or recession in the economy. With less money around to spend, fewer items can be produced, so there are fewer jobs.

20 Causes of unemployment

Technological (People whose jobs are taken over by new machinery or automation.)

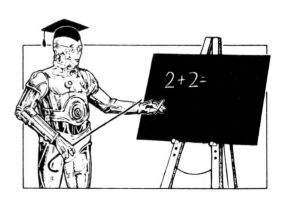

Structural (People whose jobs have been made irrelevant by a change in the structure of the economy.)

Cyclical (People whose job is caught in a slump when no one can afford to buy their goods or services.)

SOLUTIONS TO UNEMPLOYMENT

1. *Technological unemployment*. The introduction of new work practices which would mean redundancies have, in some cases, been resisted. For example, the newspaper industry has had problems in persuading unions to allow the widespread use of computers and word processors. Attempts are made to retrain some workers who have been made redundant, to give them a new skill. Job sharing and deliberate overemploying with the use of new technology can artificially keep unemployment down.

2. *Structural unemployment*. Governments have at times accepted the need to prop up part of the economy or an industry, perhaps with the use of subsidies to keep a factory open. Restrictions on imports (by means of quotas or barriers) might give British-made goods a better chance in a highly competitive market, but there might be corresponding barriers erected against British exports. Special incentives are created to encourage firms to provide jobs in areas badly hit by unemployment (Special Development Areas and Enterprise Zones).

3. *Cyclical unemployment*. The ideal solution is to even out the booms and slumps in the economy by ensuring that the good times are not too good and the bad times not too bad. Unfortunately much of this is outwith the control of the government or British industry, since the slump is likely to be world-wide. A more realistic policy would be to make sure that more money was available for people to spend, thus raising the demand for goods and services. This could be done by lowering taxation, thus putting more money into consumers' pockets, or by the government spending money on ventures such as the Youth Training Scheme.

For most of these possible solutions to happen the government would have to take positive action. Increasingly it has been seen as the government's role to intervene in the running of the economy, although political parties disagree about how much intervention is justified. Most politicians believe that full employment is a desirable long-term aim, if people can be usefully and efficiently employed. There is, however, some disagreement about whether, for the good of the country as a whole, any job is better than no job.

CASE STUDY: Placing the Blame

Mr Boyd used to work in a small factory making skateboards; then they went out of fashion and the factory closed. Mrs Boyd had been a cook at the local school. Cutbacks in local government spending meant her job had to go. And the introduction of the new cafeteria 'snack' lunch system meant there was very little real cooking to be done as most of the food was quickly reheated in microwave ovens.

Money was tight for the Boyd family as they tried to come to terms with the fall in their standard of living. Dependent on Social Security Benefits, they had no money to spare for new clothes, entertainment or 'luxury' foods such as steak.

When their son Gary left school, he couldn't find work in the area. Most of his school friends were in the same situation: living at home on Supplementary Benefit. Mr Boyd encouraged Gary to try to get a place on a Youth Training Scheme (YTS). The leaflets explained that this was a year-long programme of planned work experience linked with training or education. But there was no guarantee of a proper job at the end of the year. Gary decided to try for a place on YTS even though the money was not much more than what he received in Supplementary Benefit.

The local newspaper interviewed the Boyd family, and wrote an article about them as 'a typical unemployed family'. But when the article appeared, the Boyds were not pleased. It made them look like lazy scroungers. The reporter had got it all wrong. It wasn't their fault they had lost their jobs. And there were millions like them. Did nobody realise that they were a decent family prepared to work hard – if only even one of them could get a job. Why hadn't the reporter considered whether the government was to blame? Surely it was part of the government's job to find work for the unemployed?

Questions

1. Why will there always be some unemployment?
2. Why is unemployment a 'bad thing'?
3. What are the main causes of unemployment?
4. What can the government do to try to reduce unemployment? Are these measures likely to be successful?
5. In what ways did Mr Boyd's views on unemployment differ from those of the newspaper reporter?
6. How and why does the Youth Training Scheme operate?

Inflation

Inflation is the increase in price of goods and services as a result of a fall in the buying power of money. To most people it means they cannot buy as much as they used to.

21 The rate of inflation

22 A typical shopping basket

Item	Price (pence) 1975	1978	1984
1 doz. eggs	35	50	96
1 pint milk	$4\frac{1}{2}$	12	23
white loaf	$13\frac{1}{2}$	$21\frac{1}{2}$	35
450g butter	28	54	90
200g jar coffee	$73\frac{1}{2}$	215	229
125g tea	10	$25\frac{1}{2}$	35
6 chocolate biscuits	18	27	35
450g cheddar cheese	42	78	99
E3 size washing powder	28	$55\frac{1}{2}$	79
400g tin tomato soup	$11\frac{1}{4}$	15	31
450g pork sausages	$33\frac{1}{2}$	$47\frac{1}{2}$	72
450g mince	42	58	90
450g brussels sprouts	10	14	29
450g whiting	49	94	40
225g margarine	9	$12\frac{1}{2}$	28
1 bottle orange squash	23	$27\frac{1}{2}$	52
1 tin peaches	19	25	30
large tube toothpaste	12	30	63

The Retail Price Index is used as a measure of inflation. The cost of purchasing a 'basket' or collection of goods, including food, clothing, plus housing and transport costs, is calculated each month. Over months and years, this shows the change in the buying power of the pound.

THE EFFECTS OF INFLATION

● People are able to buy less when prices are rising fast, so fewer people are needed to produce things. This leads to unemployment.
● People who live on fixed incomes which cannot be easily raised, such as pensioners, find it increasingly difficult to make ends meet. This can lead to great hardship for many.
● If British-made goods become more expensive to sell, then exporting British goods becomes more

21 The rate of inflation

difficult, unless other countries have a high rate of inflation as well. Moreover, people in Britain may start to buy foreign-made goods if they are cheaper.
● If inflation becomes very bad (hyper-inflation), with prices rising extremely quickly, the public may lose all confidence in the use of money. Money might even cease to be used altogether, and people will only be able to get goods in exchange for other goods, by bartering.

CAUSES OF INFLATION

Three main causes of inflation can be identified. Firstly, when the cost of producing something increases, these increases may be passed on to the consumer in the form of higher prices if they cannot be paid for out of profits (cost-push inflation). For example, if the price of oil is raised then the price of plastics (made from oil) might be pushed up. Similarly, if the wages paid to the workers who produce certain goods rise, the price of the goods might have to rise to meet the increased cost in production.

Secondly, increased demand for a product pushes prices up, as does a shortage in supply (demand-pull inflation). When more people want to buy an article than there are articles available, prices rise. For example, in winter, strawberries are rare, so their price is high, but during the 'strawberry season' they are plentiful and their price will be much lower.

Another kind of inflation can occur if the government allows more money to become available (money-supply inflation). For example, the government could print more money so that everyone had more, or could allow people to borrow more money to be paid back later. With more money around, there would be too much money chasing too few goods, and this increased demand would force prices up.

SOLUTIONS TO INFLATION

1. *Cost-push inflation*. It might be possible to avoid paying more for raw materials which have gone up in price, either by using cheaper raw materials or by replacing expensive imported ones with domestic alternatives (e.g. North Sea oil instead of Middle East oil). Limits to wage increases can be organised by the government. These can take the form of statutory or compulsory wage limits, or voluntary limits where guidelines or suggestions are made and agreed on. If workers asking for higher wages realised that their wage increase would become someone else's price increase, they might accept that no one can win in the battle for higher standards of living. Alternatively the government could give people more money so that they did not need such large wage increases, for example by reducing income tax or VAT. This would give consumers more money in their pockets. Encouragement could be given to firms to invest in cost-reducing methods and find other ways to increase efficiency.

23 Causes of inflation

Money supply
More money becomes available to people so they are prepared to spend more to buy the same goods

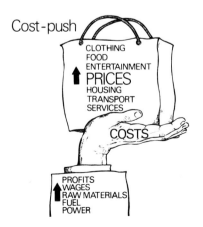

Cost-push

CLOTHING
FOOD
ENTERTAINMENT
↑ PRICES
HOUSING
TRANSPORT
SERVICES

COSTS

PROFITS
↑ WAGES
RAW MATERIALS
FUEL
POWER

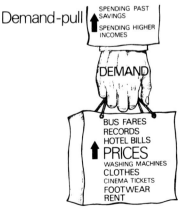

Demand-pull

↑ SPENDING PAST SAVINGS
↑ SPENDING HIGHER INCOMES

DEMAND

BUS FARES
RECORDS
HOTEL BILLS
↑ PRICES
WASHING MACHINES
CLOTHES
CINEMA TICKETS
FOOTWEAR
RENT

2. *Demand-pull inflation.* Ways have to be found to restrict the amount of money that people have to spend. Encouraging saving rather than spending, by increasing interest rates, can help. Finding ways to make it harder to spend money would have the same effect: for example; restricting hire purchase agreements by increasing the minimum deposit and raising the interest rate. This might make people more reluctant to take up such agreements. Cutting government spending on roads, education, defence can all keep money out of the pockets of consumers.

3. *Money-supply inflation.* The Bank of England can be prevented from printing more money than the country can afford to have in circulation. The government itself might make sure it does not spend more than it has, by borrowing less and spending less. A credit squeeze can be arranged so that people find it harder to borrow money.

CASE STUDY: Gladrags Co-operative

Wayne Clark started his own business in the 1960s making fashion clothes to sell from his market stall. As business expanded, he bought a shop and eventually had 30 people working for him: 'one big happy family' he thought, until the late 1970s when they asked for a wage increase and he said 'No'. They were asking for far too much and he told them so. It was more than he and the business could afford and the government had stressed the need for low pay increases. Wayne told his workers this, saying higher wages could only be paid if sales increased, so the workers agreed not to strike.

Unfortunately sales did not increase, partly because Wayne was forced to increase his prices. Some of the raw materials that he had to import (cloth and trimmings) had gone up in price so he had to increase the price of the garments made with these. Energy prices, rates, insurance all cost more. And many of his main competitors caught up with him because they had started more recently and used more up-to-date machinery. Jim laid some of his workforce off, and arranged a productivity deal with the rest. This, at least, kept him in business.

His wife was always saying that money didn't buy as much as it used to. Couldn't Wayne give himself a bigger wage? Wayne pointed out that this wouldn't be fair. He had spent months telling his workers to 'tighten their belts'. His family would have to do the same and have a lower standard of living too. There was a big row the

night Wayne's son lost his job at the local car factory. Mrs Clark thought Wayne should take him on in the shop. Wayne thought this was senseless. His workforce was cut down to 15 and with the car factory laying off workers, who could afford to buy new clothes? Bills were piling up, bankruptcy was just around the corner, and now there were arguments at home too.

Wayne had been to see his bank manager to ask for an extension to his loan, with no success. But his wife had met an old friend, who was now working for a co-operative firm. Perhaps this was the answer.

The friend explained that, since unemployment was very high, workers were interested in job security rather than higher wages. If they all joined together and took a share of the business everyone would be on the same side, and sacrifices would be more acceptable. A lawyer helped sort out the best deal available, with government help. Within two months, the new firm 'Gladrags Co-operative' was in business: slimmer, more efficient, and more united; ready to meet the challenges of controlling costs and increasing sales in their own firm.

Questions

1. How is inflation measured?
2. Why is inflation a 'bad thing'?
3. What are the main causes of inflation?
4. What can the government do to try to reduce inflation? Are these measures likely to be successful?
5. How can inflation affect a business like Wayne Clark's?
6. Look at the shopping basket table. Which items have increased most in price?
7. What can an individual do to reduce the effects of inflation?

The Balance of Payments

The Balance of Payments of a country is the difference between the cost of everything it buys from abroad (imports) and the cost of everything it sells abroad (exports). If we pay more for foreign goods and services than we receive from abroad for our goods and services we have a Balance of Payments deficit. If, on the other hand, we export more than we import, we have a Balance of Payments surplus.

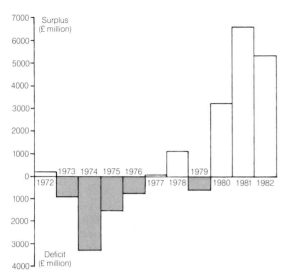

24 UK Balance of Payments 1972–82

Just as an individual wants to have money in the bank rather than have an overdraft, so any country will want to be in surplus, and it is the duty of a government to encourage people to create a surplus.

THE EFFECTS OF A DEFICIT

If a country spends more than it earns, then it is in danger of bankruptcy.

Britain is traditionally a trading nation. We do not have sufficient quantity or variety of raw materials (including food) to support ourselves, so we have to import them, usually in exchange for manufactured goods and services such as insurance and shipping.

If Britain expects to be able to sell goods and services to other countries, then these countries expect to be able to sell us goods and services in return, especially if the goods are cheaper or better than our own.

CAUSES OF A DEFICIT

1.*Too many imports.* Few countries have the full range of food and raw materials, so they must trade. However, if these imports of raw materials rise in price, they must still be paid for, to keep the British industries that use them active. Britain also imports many manufactured goods and, as these improve in quality and price, they become preferred to British-made goods.

2.*Too few exports.* Britain was traditionally good at exporting goods. But fierce competition in foreign markets from other countries has made British goods harder to sell. Traditional exports such as textiles, ships and technology have declined in the face of this competition, and many of these goods are no longer in such great demand abroad. High rates of inflation in Britain have made our exports increase in price faster than competitors' and the task of selling abroad has become harder because of this.

SOLUTIONS TO A DEFICIT

1.*Too many imports.* The obvious solution is to limit imports, especially where there is a suitable British alternative. But British consumers might prefer the foreign-made goods, and other countries might retaliate by limiting the goods they import from us, so overall Britain would be no better off. Making British goods more competitive so that people did not want to buy foreign-made ones would be a better answer. 'Buy British' campaigns often have a short-term success. It has been suggested that some goods, particularly those which are traditional and vital to the economy, should be subsidised. In this way their price would be more competitive.

2.*Too few exports.* The use of government subsidies would also improve the sales of British goods abroad. Tax concessions and investment incentives might be encouragements for export industries. If industry can be more efficient, in terms of quality, price and things like better delivery dates and after-sales service, exports might offset essential imports.

Questions

1. What is meant by a country's Balance of Payments?
2. Why does a country try to have a Blance of Payments surplus?
3. What are the main causes of a deficit?
4. What can the government do to try to maintain a Balance of Payments surplus?
5. What effect might a government's attempts to solve a Balance of Payments problem have on an individual?

Steering the Economy

In many ways the economy of a country can be regarded as a ship which has to be steered on a safe course through many hazards. The levers in Fig. **25** show the sorts of factors that governments can use to alter the course of the economy.

Unfortunately, although pulling a lever might improve the reading on one dial, it might also cause another dial to move in the wrong direction. For example, if inflation is too high the government might consider restricting wage increases. But this might give people relatively less money to spend, which might result in higher unemployment. Or, to raise the GNP, the government might consider paying people higher wages or incomes, but this would result in inflation. Moreover, when a government takes an economic decision, this may also have political consequences, making the government more or less popular with the electorate.

Check for yourself how the economy works. Suppose that prices are rising too fast. Decide which of the levers to move, and in which direction. Now consider each of the dials to see what effect this measure would have on them. Then consider which lever to move next to try to get the needles on the dials back where you want them. By trying various solutions to various problems, you may begin to realise why steering the economy is not an easy task!

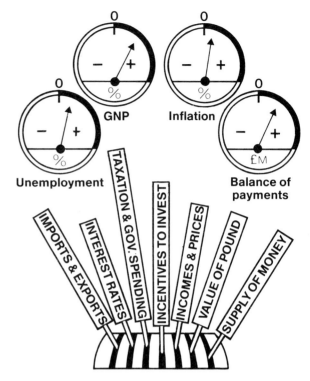

25 Steering the economy

Questions

1. Why do governments find it difficult to achieve a high and steady rate of growth?
2. What are the rewards for a government that successfully handles economic problems?
3. Describe what happens when a country decides that reducing inflation is its highest priority. Mention which 'levers' should be moved and what would happen to the 'dials'.

58

4. Industrial Relations

Trade Unions

A trade union is a group of workers who have joined together to achieve fair conditions of employment. Over 50% of people employed in Britain find it worth while to join a union.

REASONS FOR JOINING A UNION

● To be able to negotiate the best possible conditions in one's workplace: for example holidays with pay, shorter working hours, bonuses, overtime pay, safety regulations, higher basic wages.
● For job security. Control of apprenticeships and new entrants to the trade, as well as consultation over redundancy may prevent unemployment of members.
● To prevent victimisation of individual members. This is achieved by 'strength through unity' or safety in numbers.
● To ensure benefits for workers who are not at work because of sickness, injury, age or strike action.
● To get equal pay for men and women workers, maternity leave for mothers, etc.
● To negotiate adequate training for members through night school, evening classes, day release, etc.
● To provide legal backing and advice for members.
● To have some political power.

REASONS FOR NOT JOINING A UNION

● Many better-off workers consider union membership necessary.
● Some workers are in industries which are hard to organise: for example, shop workers.
● Some workers do not need the protection of a union: for example, the self-employed, workers in small-scale firms who can speak to a sympathetic owner.
● It is possible to get some of the advantages of union membership without actually joining: for example, union-negotiated wage rises are given to all.
● Some employees refuse to recognise or deal with unions.
● Some people have conscientious objections to the principle of unionism.

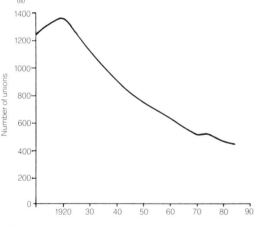

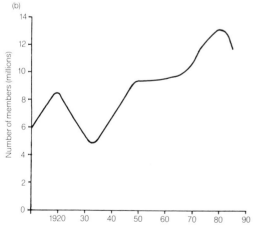

27 (a) Number of trade unions in the UK
    (b) Trade union membership
        (Source: *Department of Employment Gazette*)

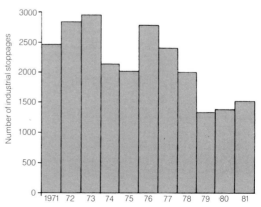

28 (a) Number of industrial stoppages

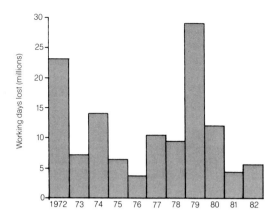

(b) Working days lost through strikes
   (Source: *Annual Abstract of Statistics*)

TYPES OF UNION

Craft Unions are the oldest and smallest unions. Members are skilled workers: for example, musicians or locomotive drivers (ASLEF). Membership may fall as the skill dies out.

Industrial unions have a very strong position when they represent most or all of the workers in an industry: for example, miners (NUM). Negotiations with employers may be easier as the union has previously settled its claims for different kinds of workers internally.

General unions take members from a variety of occupations, which sometimes makes it difficult to represent the differing interests of members. they have many unskilled members, as in TGWU and GMWU, for example.

White-collar unions, which are for office workers, professional people, government officials and clerical workers, are the fastest-growing type of union. Until recently many of their members did not consider unions to be helpful to people in their position: for example, many shop assistants felt they could negotiate with their employer without joining USDAW.

HOW A UNION IS RUN

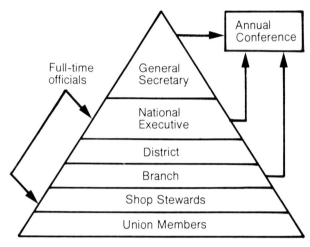

30 How a union is run

Membership. From a total population in Britain of 56 million, 21 million are in full-time employment. Of these, 11 million are members of a trade union. Some are deeply involved in their union's activities, many pay their subscriptions but do nothing more.

Shop stewards. A shop steward is usually the first person a member has contact with. They are unpaid, and elected by fellow members. Their duties may include recruitment of new members, collection of subscriptions, checking on working and safety conditions, providing a link between union officials and members, conveying the views of workers to management and negotiating on behalf of members in the local workplace.

29 International comparison of industrial disputes days lost per 1000 employees (figures are for mining, manufacturing, construction and transport industries only)

	1973	1974	1976	1979	1981	1972–81 (average)
Canada	1660	2550	2550	1660	1880	1881
France	330	250	420	360	170	285
India	1330	2480	830	2180	–	1659
Italy	2470	1800	2310	2560	950	1752
Japan	210	450	150	40	20	171
Netherlands	330	–	10	190	20	81
Sweden	10	30	20	20	60	244
UK	570	1270	300	2420	330	1045
USA	750	1480	1190	890	640	977
W. Germany	40	60	40	40	10	59

(Source: *Department of Employment Gazette*)

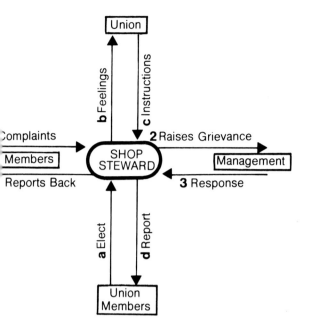

31 The role of the shop steward

TRADES UNION CONGRESS (TUC)

The TUC is the centre of the trade union movement in Britain: 92% of all trade unionists in Britain belong to unions affiliated or linked to the TUC. It aims to improve the economic and social conditions of working people and deals with trade union issues nationally and internationally.

The annual congress is held every September. At this meeting a General Council is elected. It carries out congress decisions and gives the government the trade union viewpoint on economic, social and industrial issues.

There is a liaison committee between the TUC and the Labour Party which discusses policies on industrial relations and the problems of the economy.

The General Secretary of the TUC is in some ways a spokesperson for all workers, just as the leader of the Confederation of British Industry (the employers' version of the TUC) is the spokesperson for all managers.

Branch and District. The Branch is the basic unit in the structure of a union. It admits new members, elects delegates to attend union conferences, discusses and approves wage agreements, and organises union affairs in the area. The District controls the running of branches in the area.

National Executive. These are the recognised leaders of the union. They are elected by the members and are responsible for national wage negotiations. They call for the beginning or end of official industrial action.

General Secretary. The General Secretary is a full-time official, usually elected for life. He or she is involved in day-to-day running of the union on a national level, including national negotiations with employers, and is the spokesperson for the union to the media and the government.

Full-time officials. They try to help the shop steward in the day-to-day running of union business. They are skilled negotiators, are sometimes elected to the job, but do not earn a high salary.

Annual Conference. This is held every year and Branches send delegates to represent them. Major policy decisions are made after debates on motions presented by Branches or by the National Executive. Voting is usually on a 'card vote'. Other decisions are taken during the year by the National Executive on the basis of assumptions of ordinary members' wishes, or after a ballot.

32

	EMPLOYERS	EMPLOYEES
SIDES AND SUPPORTERS	shareholders management board of directors Confederation of British industry	workers shop stewards trade union officials Trades Union Congress
	Labour Party Conservative Party	
AIMS	lower costs higher profits greater output increased efficiency	higher wages better conditions shorter hours fringe benefits
	productivity	
WEAPONS (threat or action)	lock out redundancy lay-offs overtime ban strikebreakers	strike work-to-rule work-in overtime ban picketing

Questions

1. What is a trade union?
2. Imagine you are a shop steward trying to recruit new members. What arguments would you use to persuade people to join your union? (Mention: pay, conditions, political power, etc.) What arguments would you expect to hear against joining?

3. What has happened to (a) the number of unions; (b) the membership of unions in the UK in recent years?
4. Refer to Table 29. Is the UK's reputation for a high strike rate justified? Give reasons for your answer.
5. Which kinds of union activities will an ordinary member be most involved in?
6. How does a union take decisions at (a) shop-floor level; (b) national level?
7. Explain why a shop steward can be called a 'linkperson'.
8. Why does a union need full-time officials?
9. What work does the TUC do?
10. What does the Confederation of British Industry do?

Collective Bargaining

CASE STUDY: Dispute at Brightlite

Brightlite make electric light bulbs for home use and for many other industries. They sell to supermarkets, the car industry, toymakers and fridge manufacturers. They have several factories, each making one type of bulb.

For many years they have had little trouble with industrial relations. There is only one union involved in their factories, and communications between workers and their union and the management have been good until now.

Inflation has made prices rise and the workers are complaining that their take-home pay is not high enough. They are asking for a 15% pay rise. When the shop steward told the management representative of this, he was told there was no way the management could meet this demand. The shop steward contacted his union headquarters and had some full-time officials visit the factory to talk to the management on behalf of the workers.

The shop steward is reporting on this meeting to the union at the end of the lunch break.

Ann: This meat's like rubber. For the price we pay you'd think we'd get better than this. What's your fish like, Phil?
Phil: Not bad. Chips are awful though. Quiet. Here's the shop steward. I want to know what happened this morning.
Shop steward: Right, let's call the meeting to order. We have a problem here. You know the bosses wouldn't listen to me when I tried to get an extra 15% for you, so I asked the **collective bargaining** experts to talk to them. Well, our full-time officials have been negotiating for us with the management . . .
Phil: Did we get the money?
Shop steward: Patience, patience! They've offered us 5% So what I have to ask you is: do you accept the management's offer or do we keep on pushing for 15%? Do you want to think about it or will we go straight to a vote?
Members: Vote! Vote!
Shop steward: OK. All those for 5% raise your hands. (*Counts the few hands.*) Thank you. Now all those in favour of sticking to our original demand for 15% please show. (*Counts many more hands.*)
Members: We're with you Bob!
Shop steward: Now, this means we will have to take some kind of industrial action to show the bosses we mean business. I'll tell you what the choices are and we can vote on it. First, we could keep talking to the management maybe with a conciliator?
Members: No! No!
Shop steward: OK. The management obviously aren't going to offer us any more so we might ask someone to arbitrate for us.
Phil: What's that?
Shop steward: Arbitrate? We call in someone who isn't involved and who is trusted by both sides to give a fair decision. We agree to stick to what he or she decides.
Phil: Like a referee or umpire? I'm not having that, I've seen some terrible referees in my time.
Shop steward: You may be right, Phil, and anyway, we should show them we're serious. We could have a work-to-rule where we only do what we are supposed to do and no extras.
Ann: Like the railway guards checking all the doors on the train at every station? Holding up all the other trains?
Shop steward: Yes. We'd still get paid, but maybe it's not drastic enough?
Phil: We could always have a go-slow. Do the usual job only take ages to do it.
Shop steward: Can you go any slower, Phil?!
Ann: I think we should occupy the factory. Have a sit-in, but keep working as well, and try to shame the management into giving in. We'd get publicity from the television.
Shop steward: That might work. Certainly we can't have an overtime ban since we don't have overtime. So it's either a work-in, or what I thought someone would have suggested long ago – a strike – a withdrawal of labour. We could either do it right away and . . .

As the shop steward said at the beginning of the meeting, 'We have a problem here.' In fact, there are several problems.

To start with it looks as though there is little communication between the workers and management in the factory, otherwise the dispute might have been settled without having to involve full-time officials. The management might have offered to improve conditions of work (such as the quality and price of canteen food) even if they could not offer more money.

The fact that the workers are thinking of taking industrial action shows that negotiations are not going well: perhaps the people involved are not very experienced negotiators. Or each side may feel it will lose face if it gives in to the other's demands. Often the people involved have an image of the other side which makes it difficult for them to see the other's point of view. For example, the workers may imagine the managers to be wealthy, moneygrabbers who don't care what happens to their workers, while the management may think the workers do very little work and only want to cause trouble.

Often restrictions are put on free **collective bargaining**: negotiations between management and union with no interference. The government may have passed laws to regulate collective bargaining, or it may have placed a limit of some sort on the wage rises which can be offered.

The effects of industrial action are wide ranging. A strike will mean that the workers lose money, the management and the firm will lose money and probably future orders too. Other factories which use the factory's products may have to lay off workers if they are short of light bulbs. The workers' families will also suffer. If it is an offical strike they will get some money as strike pay from the union, but if it is unofficial they will only receive Supplementary Benefit. Obviously families paying mortgages or hire-purchase payments as well as food and fuel bills will be badly affected and have to spend their savings. But the effects of industrial action are wider. The whole country is damaged: less is produced, so less is sold, (perhaps for export). Our reputation abroad suffers: foreigners will be less likely to place orders with British companies if they think the firm is likely to have a strike and so delay delivery.

The management of Brightlite hold a meeting to discuss the dispute and the threat of industrial action.

Chairman of the Board: How did your meeting with the union go, James?

James: Not very well, I'm afraid. They are insisting on 15%. I tried to explain to them that we just do not have that sort of money, and anyway the government have said no-one should get more than 5%. But they said other firms were managing better deals than we were offering, and started talking about industrial action.

Chairman: The last thing we want is industrial action of any type. Even a work-to-rule would cut our production rate and lose us orders.

James: Can't we give them 10%? They started talking about our works across the town and how they were thinking of holding a joint meeting.

Manager: No! We certainly can't give them more than the government limit. You know what they did to Jones down the road. No more government contracts, no more government grants. We can't afford that. We'll just have to try harder here and alert our other factories so that a joint deal is worked out, before they send out the pickets.

Chairman: I suppose if things really reach deadlock we could contact the Advisory, Conciliation and Arbitration Service. They did an excellent job for McBride's Engineering—came to a decision which suited both sides, and no working time lost. I think it is because ACAS are independent.

Manager: That is a bit drastic. Surely there's more talking that can be done. What about offering as much money as possible and some worker participation in running the firm . . . say a seat on the board for one of the staff?

James: Yes, I think they would jump at that. The union has been on at me for some time about doing something about the Bullock Report on Worker Participation.

Chairman: That's the first I've heard of it. Really, James, it is your job to negotiate with the union and tell us what they are thinking so that we can avoid trouble. If you had done your job properly we might not be in this situation now.

James: Sorry, I didn't think.

Manager: No good apologising now, let's see if you've forgotten to tell us anything else. It's not a political strike is it? Not set up by someone to get publicity for someone or something? You haven't dismissed a worker for not wearing a tie and are going to tell us we'll be up before an Industrial Tribunal?

James: No, nothing else. The strike is just about

money . . . and conditions too.

Chairman: What conditions?

James: The canteen is . . . Well, would you eat there?

Manager: There are no laws broken. The place is clean and no-one has become ill.

James: But there are no laws about tough meat, and dull menus. The price, too, is a bit steep — especially since there's nowhere else for them to eat.

Chairman: We might have an answer here, now let's just . . .

It looks as though the dispute at Brightlite is nearly over. The management has found what looks like being a solution to the problem: an improved canteen and as much money as they can offer.

In the future, though, James will have to be trained to carry out his job as negotiator in a more skilled way and to inform his colleagues of progress and problems. The appointment of a worker to the Board of Directors might help communications and iron out problems in the future if, say, a new machine were to be introduced. Management would be aware of the problems it might create before the introduction, if their worker board member is involved in early discussions.

They are lucky that, at least so far, the Press, radio and television have not spotlighted the dispute. Usually the publicity gained does no harm, but sometimes the story is distorted and side issues become more important than the main cause of the dispute.

Questions

1. Read the introduction to 'Dispute at Brightlite again, and look at Table **32**. What would the aims of the management and workers in the Brightlite factory be?
2. What reasons might the workers give for wanting a 15% pay rise?
3. What could they do to try to get what they want?
4. What can the management do to try to get what they want?
5. Who will suffer if there is a strike at Brightlite?
6. What had James, the management's negotiator done which made the dispute harder to solve?
7. What settlement might be reached between the management and workers at Brightlite?
8. How might the government have helped them reach a settlement?
9. What view do some members of the general public have of workers taking industrial action? Why might they have this view?

Laws and Government Action

Particularly since the early 1960s, governments have felt that they had a right, and at times a duty, to become involved in relations between employers and employees. If the aims of safety, equality peacefulness and fairness apply to society, they must also apply in industry and in workplaces. There are laws, therefore, to deal with areas such as health and safety at work, equal pay, peaceful

Letters to the Glenforth Courier

Sir – Once again the workers are not working. It's the unions to blame. They don't need an excuse to go on strike these days. Not enough money they say. How would they like to live on a pension, that's what I would like to know.

The unions have too much say in the running of the country for my liking. They can hold the management of a good firm like Brightlite to ransom just because they are greedy for money.

It's time the government did something about it. Why not make strikes illegal and put the lot of them in jail? Get the workers working for a change. I know for a fact that all the workers at Brightlite want to do night shift because they can sleep all the time.

Fred Hamilton

Sir – My husband is one of the workers at Brightlite, and is involved in the dispute. I was really angry when I read Mr Hamilton's letter and would like to reply to some of his comments.

First of all, the workers at Brightlite want a rise because, compared with other industrial workers in the town, they are poorly paid and work in poor conditions. I'm sure Mr Hamilton would not like to work in the noise of the factory or eat in the canteen there.

If the unions were not

there, bad managers c do what they liked – pa workers very little, hire fire workers when they l Workers have to thank unions for the good wor conditions most of have today.

Perhaps if the mana and people like Mr Ha ton thought a bit more fully about what it is li work in a factory all the they wouldn't say silly th like 'make strikes illegal spread nasty rumours a sleeping on night shift.

Judith Be

64

33 Nurses picket outside Greenwich Hospital, 1978

picketing, dismissal and discrimination. A government becomes involved in industrial relations to protect the rights of individuals, to prevent harassment, and to ensure that laws to do with work are upheld.

A government must also serve the interests of the public if they are likely to be affected by an industrial relations disagreement. The government can step in itself, or in some other way make sure that a settlement is reached with as little effect on outsiders and consumers as possible.

The government has a responsibility for the national economy and so must try to stop disputes which might affect it badly. As 'manager of the economy', the government aims for low unemployment, low inflation, a high Balance of Payments surplus, and steady growth. It can be expected to act if its plans are likely to be upset by a major disagreement. Where an industrial dispute threatens the jobs of the workers involved, or the jobs of others, a government may make an attempt to prevent closure or redundancies.

Governments often want to be able to control the rate of wage increases, since this can affect price increases. Workers ask for higher wages partly to keep pace with price increases and this in turn can increase prices in an upward spiral. Some of the attempts to control wages have been 'statutory' (legally binding), others have been 'voluntary' (a matter of agreement between government, unions and employers). Labour governments have, on the whole, relied on their special relationship with the union movement to issue guidelines and requests for restraint in wage demands. In the past, a Conservative government attempted to enforce

limits on wage increases, but these were largely unsuccessful. The Conservative Government from 1979 therefore tended to detail what it expected as wage settlement limits. In this way, it was able to enforce a wage settlement through the workforce it employed directly in the public sector and indirectly in local authorities. It encouraged employers in the private sector to ensure they followed the same restrictions on wage demands. The success of this method has been claimed to be due to the pressure which workers feel through the threat of unemployment if they do not reach an agreement quietly within Government limits.

Increasingly, however, governments of both the major parties have seen it as their duty to ensure that there is a balance between both sides of industry (Fig. 32). Where a government feels that power has swung too much in one direction, it will use legislation to redress the balance between the rights and the responsibilities of employers and trade unions. Generally it has been the practice for Labour governments to protect the trade unions and the rights of the individual, while Conservative governments protect employers and the rights of the individual.

● *1971 Industrial Relations Act* (Conservative) Collective agreements between employers and employees were to be binding by law; trade union rules were to be supervised; some **industrial relations** practices were defined as unfair (e.g. the closed shop where a worker must be a member of a union); a 60-day 'cooling-off' period and a ballot of members was to take place before a strike.

This law was bitterly opposed by the trade union movement, who resented interference in their affairs and the implication that they were in the wrong when there was a dispute.

● *1974 and 1976 Trade Union and Labour Relations Act* (Labour) This has repealed most of the 1971 Act, as promised at the election. Collective agreements were no longer legally binding. Peaceful picketing (attempting to persuade other workers to join a strike) became legal and pickets could not be sued by employers. The Act also stated what each side was expected to do when negotiating; it allowed a worker to complain against unfair dismissal; and made it unfair to sack workers because of their trade union activities.

Much of this legislation protected individual workers from their employers. Many employers resented what they saw as the increased power of trade unions to stop them doing what they wanted with their own workforce without the agreement of the workers.

● *1975 Employment Protection Act* (Labour) The Advisory Conciliation and Arbitration Service (ACAS) was set up. As an independent body, it was to try to help settle disputes during collective bargaining. The Act also provided more security of employment for individuals and extended the rights of workers claiming unfair dismissal.

Since then, ACAS has often been invited to help in a disagreement and has a sound record of fairness and success.

● *1980 Employment Act* (Conservative) This encouraged the wider use of secret ballots before a strike could begin or end. Trade union officials were also to be elected by this method. Lawful picketing was restricted to the worker's own place of work (secondary picketing, 'blacking' and sympathetic strikes were restricted). If workers did not wish to join a union on the grounds of conscience, then, even if there was a closed shop, they no longer had to. A Code of Practice showed how picketing and closed shops could be organised, and employers could sue a union if they suffered as a result of action that went against the code.

Trade unions saw this Act as beginning to reduce their ability to react effectively when there was a dispute. The days of the 'flying picket' (when a group of workers would move from workplace to workplace ensuring that workers joined in industrial action) were over; and the claim that, often, most of the workers called out on strike by their union leaders did not want to be on strike was about to be tested.

● *1982 Employment Act* (Conservative) This extended the restrictions on the rights of unions to enforce membership of their union through a closed shop. It allowed employers to sue a trade union for damages if it had authorised unlawful picketing, political strikes, demarcation dispute strikes, or other strikes which were nothing to do with wages or conditions of work in that workplace. Workers on strike could now be legitimately sacked.

The trade unions now saw a threat to their funds, which might have to be used to pay damages for industrial action by their members that was outwith the new narrower legal definition.

● *1984 Trade Union Act* (Conservative) The main intention in this Act was to make trade unions more democratic, and put major decisions back in the hands of ordinary members rather than their leaders. A strike would have to be approved by secret ballot of all members, or the union could be sued. The main committee and leaders of the union had to be elected by ballot. Moreover, unions would now have to ask their members, by a vote, if they

34 Workers vote on a managerial decision, Upper Clyde Shipbuilders

wanted some of their membership dues to be spent on political activities, such as donations to the Labour Party.

Trade unions claimed that nearly all of them were already democratic, even if elections were held in public. They also claimed that employers were not required to behave democratically, and that the changes to the political levy were an obvious attack on the historical links between the trade union movement and the Labour Party, designed to cripple the Conservatives' political opponents.

Questions

1. Why do governments become involved in industrial relations?
2. What is the difference between statutory and voluntary wage control?
3. What is meant by each of the following: closed shop; secret ballot; dispute; peaceful picketing; unfair dismissal; arbitration; strike; code of practice; demarcation dispute?
4. In what ways are trade unions democratic?
5. What are the links between the main political parties and trade unions and businesses?

PART 3

Society

1. Living in Great Britain

At various times in their lives people have to make decisions about how and where to live. They must ask themselves certain questions, and their different answers result in many different lifestyles.

Where to live? In town or country; in the north or south; in a flat or a house?

How to earn money? Working indoors or outdoors; self employed or wage earner; a career or part time?

What to do with the money? Spend or save?

People are very rarely able to make a completely free choice: they have to take into account various limiting factors. And all the time the government and other organisations are offering advice, giving assistance, encouraging certain decisions and preventing others.

Because of this, many people make similar decisions about where and how to live, and in this way **communities** are formed. Communities make up society.

Housing Base

In the early 1800s the great changes of the Industrial Revolution began to take place in Britain as handwork in homes was gradually replaced by machine-work in factories. Many people who lived in the countryside began to move into the towns to work in the new fast growing **industries**. Basic terraced and tenement houses were quickly built for these workers, which deteriorated to an unacceptable standard not long afterwards.

By the late 1800s, government and local authorities were worried about the unhealthy dilapidated houses that many working people lived in. Slum clearance programmes were started to demolish these houses and build more modern sanitary housing. This gradual replacement of slums continued until the 1950s, hastened in some cities by the effects of bombing during the second world war.

It became obvious that the big cities needed properly planned development. Rebuilding bit by bit in certain areas did not cure the problems facing the cities. There were still many substandard houses, few open spaces, dirty factories close to houses, and streets congested with traffic. Something had to be done to improve the city environment. Here are some of the solutions that were tried from the 1950s onwards.

SOLUTIONS TO CITY PROBLEMS

Overspill

Some large cities which were overcrowded reached agreements with smaller towns to send 'overspill' families to start a new life in these towns. Usually the newcomers were offered local authority houses and there were jobs available for them.

Redevelopment

Town planners felt that the only answer for the worst parts of some cities (often the inner-city areas) was to knock down most of the buildings and start again, this time with a plan. The newly built areas were carefully thought out, with new factories separated from housing. Small shopping centres, schools and clinics were built near the new types of housing: modern tenements and high-rise blocks of flats. Fig. **1** shows the changes that **redevelopment** can bring to an area.

Housing Schemes

Large housing schemes were built by local **authorities** on the outskirts of towns and cities to rehouse some of the families from the slums, and cater for the growing population. These provided modern tenement homes for families, and some had specially designed smaller housing units for old people.

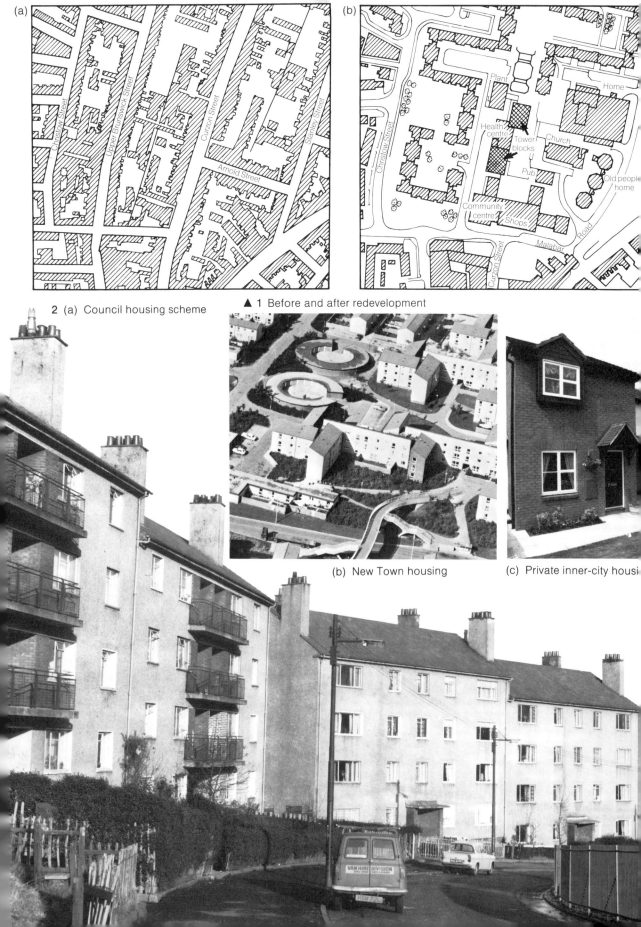

(a)

Christow Street
Upper Brunswick Street
Curzon Street
Stanley Street
Arnold Street

(b)

Plant
Home
Health centre
Tower blocks
Church
Pub
Old people home
Community centre
Shops
Malabar Road
Curzon Street

2 (a) Council housing scheme

▲ 1 Before and after redevelopment

(b) New Town housing

(c) Private inner-city housi

New Towns

Since 1946, 32 completely new towns have been designed and built (e.g. Cumbernauld, Milton Keynes). They were planned to be self-contained, with everything the inhabitants would need: jobs, shops, entertainment facilities and excitingly designed modern housing. A special feature of many New Towns is the careful separation of people and traffic, with pathways leading to the town centre. The New Towns gave planners the chance to design complete towns and get the balance right between open space, houses, shops, factories, amenities and traffic.

Private Housing

Private companies (e.g. Barratt, Wimpey) build houses and sell them to people who can buy them or who are able to afford mortgage repayments. Many estates of privately owned houses are in the suburbs, but more recently town houses and flats have been built on inner-city sites.

All these solutions have had some success but they have also produced other problems.

SOME PROBLEMS AND FURTHER SOLUTIONS

The Break-up of Families and Communities

When an area is redeveloped, it is not always possible to rehouse people near their relatives, friends and old neighbours. People who have been part of a close community in the old housing areas suddenly find themselves living in a new area among strangers. Families who have lived within streets of one another are scattered across the city. As a result, many people are reluctant to move and face the problems of settling into a new area and making new friends.

In an effort to keep communities together, many sound old buildings are now renovated so that the original inhabitants can move back once the work is complete. This improves the living conditions and keeps the community, with its local shops and businesses, together.

Where is the Glasgow?

Adam McNaughton

Oh, where is the Glasgow where I used tae stey,
The white wally closes done up wi' pipe cley;
Where ye knew every neighbour frae first floor tae third,
And tae keep your door locked was considered absurd.
Do you know the folks steying next door tae you?

And where is the wee shop where I used tae buy
A quarter o' totties, a tuppeny pie,
A bag o' broken biscuits an' three totty scones,
An the wumman aye asked, 'How's your maw gettin' on?'
Can your big supermarket give service like that?

(from *The Scottish folksinger,*
by Norman Buchan and Peter Hall
published by Collins)

Lack of Amenities

The first people to move into some New Towns complained of New Town Blues: they knew no-one, and, at this early stage of development, the New Towns had few amenities; they consisted mainly of housing. Many people on the edge of city housing estates had the same complaints but, unlike the New Town families, they had to wait a long time for some amenities. Poor shopping **facilities,** and a lack of medical centres, community halls, entertainment and sports facilities, make life in these housing schemes very difficult and was often blamed for anti-social behaviour and vandalism.

Community Spirit

In recent years many of the 'missing' facilities have been built and projects have begun to encourage people to be proud of their local area and take more care of shared property such as parks and community halls. Some areas have local festival societies producing activities for people of all ages. Others have co-operative projects to give the area things that it lacks, such as launderettes, hairdressers, nurseries, and maintenance services. Some tenants have formed management co-operatives to organise repairs, tenancy changes and improvements to their area. All these ideas give people a personal stake in their local community.

They feel it is their community and it is in their interest to look after it. Selling local authority houses to tenants at a reduced price and very basic 'wind and watertight' houses to 'homesteaders' (see the advertisement) is also thought to build the strength of community spirit.

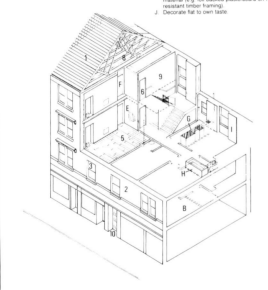

Homesteading Responsibilities

THE COUNCIL WILL UNDERTAKE THE FOLLOWING:–

1. Re-roofing, new gutters, downpipes and drainage connections.
2. External stone cleaning and stone repairs.
3. New windows.
4. Back courts landscaped with binstores and drying areas.
5. All floors and ceilings repairs.
6. New front door to each flat.
7. Supply all services (gas, water, drainage, electrical and ventilation stack). Homesteader to connect from meter point or main runs of relevant services.
8. Insulate loft.
9. Decorate close and stairwell.
10. New front and rear close doors.

THE HOMESTEADER WILL UNDERTAKE THE FOLLOWING:–

A. To obtain Building Warrant for work undertaken by Homesteader.
B. Supply and erect partitions where required (broken lines).
C. Install the electrical circuits for sockets etc., (excluding ceiling lights), connecting to consumer unit.
D. Install heating as required.
E. Plaster walls where required.
F. Complete all internal joiner work to doors, skirtings etc.
G. Design, supply and fit out new kitchen including plumberwork.
H. Design, supply and fit out new bathroom including plumberwork.
I. Line all external walls internally with suitable material (e.g. foil backed plasterboard on rot resistant timber framing).
J. Decorate flat to own taste.

3 Homesteading advert

High-rise Blocks

This type of housing was built as part of many redevelopment schemes, but was found to be unsuitable for certain groups of people. Families with young children could not let them outside to play, and keeping children indoors most of the time put great strain on family relationships. Mothers at home with young children did not meet many people and suffered loneliness and depression. Old people also found that these flats were high-rise prisons. Vandalism and breakdowns often meant that the lifts could not be used, so old people on the

4 High-rise housing

upper floors were isolated, unable to leave the building.

Local authorities no longer build these high-rise blocks. Some of the worst ones have been demolished and others refurbished to accommodate students and single people. When new housing is planned, careful thought is given to the type of families who will live in the area, and often the local people are consulted about the type of housing they would prefer.

Building Materials

Many modern buildings are made of factory-built sections that are fastened together on site. Most are well made and carefully put together, but there have been some examples of shoddy building. Bad design or careless construction can lead to dampness (although many aspects of modern living are also blamed for this), resulting in black mould on walls, peeling wallpaper, damp clothes and unusable rooms. Local authority experts say many of the 'damp' homes are not heated well enough, are not properly ventilated, and that drying clothes indoors puts too much moisture into the air. Tenants reply that they cannot afford to heat the houses, or open windows to let expensive heat escape.

Imbalances

The average age of the city dweller has risen: the people who chose to move out were young. They also tended to be the more skilled and adaptable. This makes it more difficult for cities to attract industries which would prefer a highly skilled workforce.

For many years it was local authority policy to house similar families together: large families in large houses in one area, old people in another area. There was also a tendency to house 'problem families' (who had difficulty in paying their rent or had troublesome members) together, and one-parent families together. But this was found not to be a good idea, and created many problems. Newer areas have a greater mix of housing type and people. Private builders are also being encouraged to build next to local authority housing areas to give a greater variety.

Questions

1. List the main housing problems which faced planners in the 1950s.
2. What solutions were tried for these problems?
3. Look at the maps showing redevelopment (Fig. 1). What changes did redevelopment bring?
4. What extra problems did the first solutions produce and how are they being tackled?
5. Look at the song, 'Where is the Glasgow?'. What are the writer's feelings about the city?

Deprivation

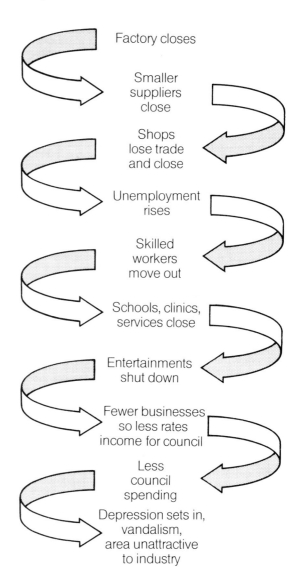

Factory closes

Smaller suppliers close

Shops lose trade and close

Unemployment rises

Skilled workers move out

Schools, clinics, services close

Entertainments shut down

Fewer businesses so less rates income for council

Less council spending

Depression sets in, vandalism, area unattractive to industry

5 The spiral of deprivation

An area of **deprivation** suffers from several problems at once: housing, industrial, social and money problems. This often comes about because one problem leads to another, progressing in a downwards spiral. Starting at any point on the spiral, things will get worse and worse (Fig. 5). If the local and the central government do nothing, the area decays and the quality of life of the people who live there drops lower and lower.

Glenforth is an imaginary place, but its problems are typical of many areas suffering deprivation.

6 Glenforth

Extract from an article in the
Glenforth Courier

It is indeed a sad day for Glenforth. The shipyard gates closed for the last time today at Young's as 1500 workers walked home jobless, or redundant as they call it now. Only 200 of them have been promised jobs in the next town in McLay's yard. They said it was rationalisation: concentrating the work in the modern yard, which is equipped to build bulk carriers instead of the famous Young's luxury liners which no-one wants any more.

The impact of the yard closing will be felt far and wide. Many other local firms will be hit. Take, for example, the firm of McKinley and Thoms. Mr Thoms Junior said today, 'This is a blow for us. Who wants to buy our propeller shafts now with Young's gone? I doubt if my workforce will have a happy Christmas this year.'

Local shopkeepers will suffer too. Those near the yard who supplied 'pieces' and soft drinks have already put up their shutters and moved. The manager of the big department store in town sees hard times ahead for his business. Who's going to buy a new three-piece suite and new clothes out of redundancy money and Social Security? Even the food shops can put away their exotic food: more bread and jam!

Many of the Campbells, McLarens and McKays whose ancestors came to Glenforth during the Highland Clearance are fed up living in Glenforth anyway. Mr Thomas Ure (60), said, 'I've lived here all my life, and it sickens me to see the changes around here. Time was you could walk the streets safely. Now you're scared to leave your house. And the houses – I remember when they were almost new and people were proud of them – wally closes and

all. Now they're almost falling down and the facilities are rotten. One toilet for every three families and hot water out of a wee geyser. I wish I could move, but who would want to take me on?'

Certainly the scene is most depressing. Idle cranes above a dirty river; smoke from the one remaining factory pouring through filthy back courts; gang slogans written on anything that stands still; political slogans written on the roads promising a new world.

It looks as though many people will try to move away from Glenforth. Those with skills should be able to find work, perhaps in the oil boom areas of the New Towns. The semi-skilled and unskilled will just have to hope for the best. Many of those who will leave are the backbone of the community – running clubs, organising the Gala week, and speaking up for the community to the Council when things go wrong. But what will happen

when they are gone? The are strong rumours that wi fewer people living in t town and fewer children seems to be young famili who move out) at least o of the schools will close. T local hospital too is threa ened with reorganisatio One or two dentists and G have already gone. All th on top of the closure of t last cinema and bingo h and all but one of the caf makes this a depressi place. Are streets of emp houses all we can hope fo The Council says it longer has the money co ing in from the rates to p for more than essential r pairs. Unless a new indust moves to the area they ca not see things getting a better. But what indust alists would want to set business in a place with n thing to offer but its pride a glorious past?

each point on the spiral of deprivation there are
ngs which central and local government, or the
ple of the area, might do to try to improve things.
Liverpool and Glasgow, attempts have been
de to break out of the spiral of deprivation.

ERPOOL, NEW SIGNS OF LIFE
THE GHETTO

rseyside, which boasts some of Britain's worst
ms, is showing the rest of the country how to
est private money to revitalise working-class
ettoes.

Myrtle Gardens was five blocks of flats built in the
30s. Although they were modernised by the
incil in 1968, they were still unattractive and
pleasant to live in.

Demolition had begun when the council arran-
d to sell them to Barratt, the private building firm.
rratt renovated the flats, provided answer
ones and a 24-hour janitor service. New flats are
be built to replace the demolished block. Now
led Minster Court, the flats should sell well as
y are near the university and city centre. The
ter-off middle classes left the city centre long ago
the suburbs; it will not be easy to entice them
ck, though Liverpool badly needs a better social
lance and Barratt is making a good try.

Cantrol Farm is one of the vast housing estates
lt around Liverpool to house tenants displaced
slum clearance. It is typical of a housing scheme
mmunity dumped miles from the city centre. The

population of 'Legoland' has declined from 12 000
to 9000. The council decided the whole estate
including land, shops and houses should be sold to
a non-profitmaking trust backed by private enterprises. The Stockbridge Village Trust will demolish
some maisonettes, renovate three tower blocks,
knock down part of the shopping centre and
redesign the housing areas. Barratt will build another 1000 houses, some for sale, some for rent.

The money comes from Barclay's Bank, the
Abbey National Building Society and the local
council. The aim is to change Cantrol Farm from a
council house ghetto to an estate with a mix of
ownership and tenancies.

GLASGOW EASTERN AREA RENEWAL
[GEAR]

In the 1970s the east end of Glasgow was identified
as suffering from multiple deprivation. Major employers in textiles and engineering had closed
down. Many families had left the area. The people
who remained faced high unemployment, and lived
in substandard crumbling homes. Crime and vandalism were serious problems. As retail businesses
moved out, people had to use the inadequate bus
and train services to visit other shopping centres. It
was obvious that, with such a range of problems
over a large area, piecemeal redevelopment would
not work successfully.

GEAR was set up in 1976 to try to revitalise this
area. The worst housing and derelict factories were

Before and after renovation in Liverpool

cleared. Other houses were modernised or re-habilitated. But the GEAR agency knew that the area needed more than refurbished houses and modern factories. Central government, local government, health, housing, employment services and the Scottish Development Agency worked together with the local people to find out what the area really needed. As a result, GEAR has, in addition to bright new factories, small workshops, and private and local authority housing: welfare rights officers, new Social Security offices, pre-school facilities; sports centres; a new police station and more police officers on the beat; door chains and viewers for the elderly in their houses; anti-vandalism projects; services to combat alcoholism; new geriatric units; improved bus services and 'shoppabuses'; community flats and tenants' meeting halls; and many other things.

Together the agencies hope to recreate the vitality and energy of the old east end.

Questions

1. What is meant by deprivation?
2. What might a government do to try to break the spiral of deprivation?
3. Using the extract from the *Glenforth Courier*, describe the effect the closure of a large firm can have on a town. Mention: other firms, shop-keepers, crime, housing, environment, social amenities, morale.

4. Choose either Liverpool or Glasgow and write a summary of attempts to break out of the spiral of deprivation.

Planning

In a country with a population of 56 million, many things need careful planning. If no group of people was employed to take an overview of where buildings were put and roads laid down, development could go badly wrong. For example, smoky factories might be placed beside houses; large housing estates might be built with no schools nearby. Government **ministers**, local authorities and government agencies do most of the planning. It is part of their job to make sure that roads and railways go where they are needed; that factories are sensibly sited and do not pollute the surrounding area; that there are enough schools and hospitals for local needs.

Planners have also begun to think carefully about the appearance of towns and industrial areas and about keeping some of the country's wild areas. Good architectural design is important, but so is variety, open space, and buildings which people like to live in and be near. The revamping of many city areas has shown that planners have come a long way from the 'city in the sky' ideas of the first redevelopment areas.

8 Air pollution

9 The mass of paperwork for the Sizewell B enquiry

The best site for, say, a new hospital is worked out by taking into account where the largest number of patients is likely to come from, the availability of flat land and local transport. But other things beyond the local area have to be considered too: how far away is the nearest other hospital? Will there be enough government money to pay for the new building? Will nursing and other staff be keen to move into the area?

In recent years there has been increasing concern (both in government and among the general public) about the effects new developments have on the surrounding area, the local environment. Scientists now know that smoke and fumes released into the atmosphere by industrial oil and coal furnaces combine with water vapour in the clouds and make the rain acid. This Acid Rain causes widespread damage to plants, animals and fish. Waste from factories and towns can kill all life in rivers, lakes and the sea; and many of the things industries use can damage people and their environment. Smokeless zones, and regulations about the use of asbestos and disposal of toxic wastes, have helped. But many development proposals are potentially harmful. A number of pressure groups (e.g. Greenpeace) are very active in making sure the government and local authorities are aware of the effect new developments might have on the environment.

Local government have a chance to become involved in plans for development in their area. When broad planning policies are drawn up (e.g. saying which areas should be industrial and which residential) these plans are advertised in newspapers and can be examined by the public at planning offices and libraries. Individuals can express their views and object to any part of the plans to the local planning authority at a public local planning enquiry. Smaller-scale proposals, such as house extensions, new buildings or new garages, have to be publicised locally and people living nearby can object and stop the proposed development. Public enquiries into major developments, such as the Sizewell B Power Station, can run for many months and cost a great deal of money as both the protesters (in this case pressure groups such as Friends of the Earth) and the developers (the Central Electricity Generating Board) hire legal experts and call on highly qualified scientific witnesses to support their case.

Stop the Traffic

Families in a narrow Glenforth street are becoming angry because more and more heavy traffic is thundering past their homes. Nearly 200 people have signed a petition asking the local council to close the street to traffic.

On of the petition organisers said, 'The road is old, narrow and runs through a housing area with lots of children. There are a number of schools and some old people's houses. Parts of the road have no pavement, and lorries roar past, in some cases only 10 feet from windows. It is only a matter of time before there is a serious accident.'

Local residents had a march on the Town Hall to show councillors how strongly they feel about this issue. They have also called in a pollution expert who told our reporter, 'Not only do the local people face problems of the possibility of accidents, but their environment is suffering. Buildings are being shaken to their foundations by the vibrations caused by heavy lorries. At times, the noise from the traffic in some of the houses is intolerable. People have to live in the rear rooms of their homes. The fumes from traffic exhausts have raised the level of lead in the air; this has been shown to damage people's health and affects children particularly · badly.'

Council officials say they know residents are unhappy and promise to look into the matter. But they say a new road by-passing the housing area is unlikely because of cost.

Nuclear Waste Storm

Land-based sites for dumping nuclear waste have been named. A storm of protest has greeted the announcement in the House of Commons.

Local residents are afraid that a disused mine under their homes is the likely storage place for the waste, and have formed an Action Committee to fight the plan. There will have to be surveys and drilling to check the site, which might need to have planning permission. Residents hope their protests will mean a public enquiry into the site.

Already, national environmental groups have condemned the 'dump' move. A spokesperson said, 'I don't think we know enough about the risks to people now or in the future from nuclear waste dumps. This material may remain harmful for thousands of years. Will the containers last that long? Just one small leak from a container could be a serious health risk to people in the area.'

A nuclear expert reassured our reporter that the residents' fears were groundless. 'Most of these scare stories are based on fear and ignorance. The greatest care will be taken in these dump areas to make sure the local people are protected. We, the people who know, are certain the waste products from our nuclear industry can be disposed of safely.'

Questions

1. What things have to be considered when a site is chosen for (a) a hospital (b) a pub?
2. What sort of things do planners and pressure groups have to take into account when thinking about any new plan?
3. What chances does a member of the public have to influence development plans for the local area?
4. If you were asked to plan a New Town, from scratch, which of these would you plan, in which order, and why? Houses; roads; factories; play areas; open spaces; schools; shops; entertainment.

Living Patterns

With 56 million people living in Britain, there are obviously many different lifestyles. Not everyone lives in an area as deprived as Glenforth; not everyone lives in a city. The following studies give some ideas of different ways of life. Obviously these are imaginary people but they reflect the lives of many real people.

LIFE ON A CROFT

Hamish and Donagh McDonald rent a small five acre croft in the Western Isles. Like other crofters they have security of tenure: they cannot lose the croft. It is part of a township of ten crofts on the shore. Their four cows graze the common land on the edge of the township and their sheep are on the nearby hills. With the thin poor soil and cool wet weather, they can't grow much: oats, potatoes and vegetables in a few small fields near the house. They make some money from milk, wool and eggs and the occasional bullock which they sell but if it wasn't for the extra income they earn from weaving work and doing bed and breakfast in the summer, they

10 A crofting community, South Uist

like so many others, would have to give up the croft.

Some of the crofts are not worked now and have been taken over as holiday houses; others are badly neglected as the crofters are too old to work the land. Hamish and Donagh's two children are the only ones in the township and they will probably not stay to run the croft. After travelling to the mainland to secondary school and tasting the 'bright lights' of town life, and a greater range of job opportunities, they are unlikely to want to spend the rest of their lives in the quiet township.

The government has tried to help the township: grants and loans are not too difficult to get to improve the land or extend houses to help with the tourist trade, but they can do nothing about the high cost of living in the islands and the remoteness of the place.

LIFE ON A PRIVATE HOUSING ESTATE

Ronnie Forbes likes nothing better than a week's work based in his home town. He doesn't mind travelling from town to town selling soap powder, but he much prefers being able to come home every evening rather than spending a few nights a week in a hotel.

He lives in a semi-detached house in an estate on the edge of a large city. After saving hard for several years, he and his wife Jill managed to get a mortgage to buy their 'dream home': it will be theirs in the year 2001!

Life on the estate is very pleasant. Most of the people are about their age and, like them, have young families. That means their childen have lots of others to play with in the large gardens and the local swing park, and Jill has lots of friendly neighbours to go to the shopping centre with. There is usually one friend who can take the rest of them in the family car. Jill also helps with the estate playgroup where their youngest child goes on two mornings a week.

Ronnie's parents live in the centre of town which means they are not too close – sometimes a good thing Ronnie thinks! He and Jill go to see them with the children every second weekend: having a company car makes it all very simple. They usually go on holiday with them too – a package to somewhere sunny – grandparents make great babysitters!

Ronnie goes to the local hotel for a drink on a Friday night with some friends from the estate – mostly young professional people like himself – there's a police officer, a teacher, a shop manager and another sales person. In the summer they usually manage a few rounds of golf. Apart from their golf handicaps, they talk about the rising crime rate (shoplifting in particular), the 'youth of today', and the rival merits of different brands of soap powder.

LIFE IN A HOUSING SCHEME

'The house is fine – central heating, our own bathroom and quite big really. It's the area I don't like. There's street after street of houses and nothing else. All the streets seem to look the same. Only a few people look after the gardens – kids run through them and paint things on walls. I don't blame them really – there is nothing for them to do – a swing park isn't much use to a a teenager. The cinema or dancing means an expensive trip into town. There's one chip shop and one youth club for hundreds of kids. You'd think the council who built this place would have realised we needed more than just houses to live in. It's true there's a big sports centre and a shopping centre opening in a year or two but we've been here ten years! The people who planned this place obviously didn't try living in it with a family – they haven't stood in the rain for half-an-hour waiting for a bus to the shops with two toddlers and a pram. Nor did they think about how much more expensive it is living out here on the edge of the town. Bus fares cost a fortune, and there are so few shops they can charge what they like . . .'

11 A housing scheme

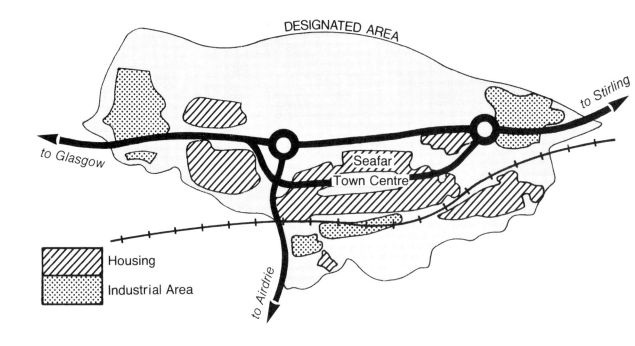

to Stirling

to Glasgow

Seafar
Town Centre

to Airdrie

Housing

Industrial Area

DESIGNATED AREA

12 Cumbernauld

LIFE IN A SCOTTISH NEW TOWN

Heather Shaw lives in Seafar, Cumbernauld, in one of the modern single-aspect houses. It took her some time to get used to living in a house with the bedroom downstairs and living room and kitchen on the first floor, but it certainly gave her pleasant views of the landscaped walkways and gardens, and no-one overlooked her house. She likes the cul-de-sac style of community housing. She soon got to know the people living in the other eight houses in the cul-de-sac and it made settling in much easier – feeling part of a small community. She also likes the walkways: she can walk to the local shops and even to work in the town centre. There are pedestrian footbridges across the main roads and traffic-free areas make it really safe for children. The neighbourhoods have small groups of shops, primary schools and medical services. The town centre provides large chain stores, banks, hotels and pubs. The sports centre is very popular. Everything in the town is just where it should be. Garages for private cars are near the houses, but the roads to them avoid the gardens, play areas and walkways. Different types and styles of houses are mixed together so that there is variety. The industrial estates are totally separate from the residential areas so there are no problems of noise or air pollution.

LIFE IN A COMMUTER TOWN

Laura and Mike Wilkinson live in a pleasant town within travelling distance of London. They wanted a house with a garden and could not afford the high house prices inside London so they decided to live within commuting distance of both their jobs.

Mike is a personnel manager with a biscuit-making firm. Usually he travels to work by train, catching a train at the local station before 8 a.m. and returning home about 7 p.m. This extra time used in travelling makes his working day long, and it is often made longer if there are delays to trains. Sometimes Mike uses his car to travel to work, but he finds the traffic jams more nerve-racking than the packed commuter trains, and the parking can be a nightmare.

Laura used to travel into London to work too, but now her firm, which makes micro-computers, has moved to a smart group of factories and offices set in the countryside. Her work in the accounting department is the same as it was when the factory and offices were in London, but the surroundings are much more pleasant with bright modern office space and attractive parks and gardens outside. Now Laura drives along country roads to work, and finds it much more relaxing and cheaper than the expensive daily train commuter trip.

Neither Laura nor Mike plays a big part in the

78

13 Commuters

community life of their town. Usually, after preparing and eating a meal, they spend what is left of the evening relaxing, reading, listening to records or watching television. They enjoy gardening and occasionally chat to neighbours on a summer evening. But they do not have friends in the town. Mike knows a few people who regularly travel in the same part of the train with him and Laura knows the local shopkeepers but they do not attend local gatherings like dances and meetings. Their friends are working colleagues whom they entertain from time to time, or together plan a theatre visit in the west end of London.

INNER CITY LIFE

Karam Chand lived and worked in Britain for 10 years before he could afford to send for his wife and children who lived in the Punjab. They have lived here for many years now: one of Karam's children and all his four grandchildren were born in Britain.

The family live in a terraced house near the centre of a large city. Most of the houses nearby are in poor condition. Some are empty and await demolition; others have been taken over by better-off families and are being renovated. But Karam and many of his neighbours cannot afford to move out of their slum houses: the rents in better property would be too high.

Life in their inner-city area can be tough. Apart from the crumbling buldings, there are still some noisy dirty workshops among the houses. Derelict land makes a do-it-yourself adventure playground for the younger children, and a meeting place for out-of-work teenagers. A lot of young people in the area are unemployed and, having nothing to do and very little money, they hang around the streets and sometimes get into trouble with the police. The high youth unemployment, poor living conditions and the racist attitudes of some white people were blamed for the inner-city riots of the early 1980s.

Since the riots, there have been local projects set up to give young people training courses and work experience. But the Chands and other families like them are concerned that these aren't enough. The

14 The inner city

	Rural (to do with villages, hamlets, isolated settlements)	Urban (to do with towns and cities)
Population	Small number of people living in small groups or isolated units. Small range of possible friends. Extended family is important.	Large number of people living close together. Wide choice of friends. 'Family' less important.
Housing	Single family houses, cottages of different ages. Owned or rented privately or may be tied to job. Gardens for vegetable growing and poultry common.	Large variety of house type and tenure. Much is local authority owned. Much is high density tower blocks or tenement flats. Gardens small and rare. Some allotments.
Education	Small one-or two-teacher village schools. Composite classes common. Secondary schooling means travelling long distance or staying away from home. Further education limited.	Local primary and secondary schools within walking distance. Usually modern and well equipped. Further education widely available.
Shopping	Village stores for most shopping. Mail order important. Mobile shops and banks necessary. Prices tend to be high. Have to go to market town for major purchases.	Local shopping centres for most shopping. Some mobile shops for housing schemes. Wide choice including cut-price supermarkets and discount stores. Near major shopping centre.
Social services	Doctor will serve area but major surgery has to be done at city hospital. Dentist at distance. Provide own care for old people, families with problems, etc.	Choice of doctors/dentists, often in modern group practices in health centres. Hospitals offer wide range of specialist services. Full range of social and welfare services available. Voluntary organisations run play groups, etc.
Work	Mainly linked to agriculture, or services such as shops, garages, post office.	Large-scale industries, factories, offices. Opportunities to train or retrain.
Transport	Public services only between larger centres. Car almost essential.	Integrated transport service. Publicly operated rail and bus network. Air travel from larger centres.
Entertainment	Generated locally, e.g. choirs, drama groups, own family. Little 'canned' entertainment. Television, radio, videos but occasionally reception may be poor.	Wide range: cinemas, discos, dance halls, clubs, football matches, sports centres, swimming pools, concerts, as well as radio, television, videos.
Environment	Fresh air, open space, quiet, generally pleasing, though may be isolated from other people.	Air pollution widespread, some parks, gardens, play spaces. Many areas very run down. Often depressing.
Crime and other social problems	Little crime or vandalism. Problems are solved by local community. Underemployment.	Crime rate high especially in bigger cities. Broken homes, single-parent families. Delinquency fairly widespread. Unemployment. Possible racial, religious and gang conflict.

whole area needs rebuilding; people need to be educated about how people from other cultures live; more social workers, teachers, health visitors, community relations workers are all needed if life in the area is to get any better.

It seems ironic that such a ghetto of poverty and despair is so close to the fashionable glossy business centre of the city. The business people don't seem to notice the poverty. Or, if they do, they don't seem to care.

Questions

1. Using the case studies in this unit, compare different living environments in Britain under these headings: housing, recreation, jobs, the future.
2. Write a short account of the living pattern in your home area. Mention: types of housing; environment; main industries; leisure facilities; the future.
3. What are the main differences between life in the countryside and life in large towns?

2. Work

16 Why work?

Looking for Work

Finding the right job is about matching your interests, abilities and talents to the type of job that suits you best (for example, office, outdoor, scientific or caring for people) and then looking to see where the opportunities for that type of job are. Job opportunities depend on demand. It is obviously more difficult to find a job in a declining industry such as shipbuilding than in an expanding or stable industry such as petro-chemicals. It is easier to find a job in an area that is short of workers (e.g. the south-east) than in an area which is short of work (e.g. Strathclyde). It is easier to find work in times of economic expansion than in times of recession. The economic recession of the 1980s means that there are not many jobs available for school-leavers, particularly in certain areas of the country. It is essential, therefore, to use the best forms of help available (e.g. the Careers Service) and to look actively for vacancies (e.g. in Job Centres, newspaper advertisements, and through friends and relatives) rather than 'waiting for something to turn up'. It is important to obtain the qualifications that will be of most use, and to make the maximum use of personal abilities and qualities.

QUALIFICATIONS

There are two sorts of qualifications: certificates awarded for school-leaving examinations, college courses, university degrees, etc.; and personal qualifications which are less easy to test, such as

17 Factors affecting choice of work

nimble fingers, neatness, colour sense, strength, as well as personality factors such as patience, the ability to take or give instruction, and initiative.

Most jobs require both sorts of qualifications. Both a brain surgeon and a transistor assembler need nimble fingers and patience, though only the surgeon will also need a university degree. All workers need good health, though it is more important for a forestry worker to be physically fit than someone who works indoors.

Some certificates are easier to obtain than others: for example, a Standard Grade or O level in French is easier to pass than a university degree in French. Examinations are designed to test particular skills at various levels of difficulty. They are useful to employers as a measure of the abilities of the candidates for a job. As well as school examinations and university degrees, there are many types of qualifications that can be studied for after leaving school: for example, City and Guild certificates, diplomas from technical colleges, VEC/SCOTVEC and other certificates. The courses for many of these provide training for professional and technical careers. Apart from these external courses, a great deal is learned on the job in apprenticeships, work experience, and major programmes for school leavers such as the Youth Training Scheme.

TYPES OF JOBS

Britain, as an advanced industrial nation, has a wide range of jobs for people to consider. The Industrial Revolution, which brought division of labour and increased specialisation, made it more likely that people would be required to settle into one line of work, rather than be able to turn their hand to many different things. However, a second 'Industrial Revolution', brought about by modern technology, indicates that many workers will have to become more adaptable, to meet the demands for new skills. They will have to be prepared to retrain several times during their working lives as their skills are no longer required and new ones are needed instead.

Jobs can be grouped in two main ways: according to where the work is done (in a factory, shop or outdoors); or according to the type of work involved (practical, intellectual, social, physical). The following case studies illustrate the wide range of jobs in which British working people are occupied. Some people are self-employed and working on their own, while at the other extreme some people work in huge factories for employers that they never see.

A Potter

Bill is a craftsman potter. He works in a workshop in his back garden and sells his pots to tourists and the local craft shop. Since he is his own boss, he can vary his hours of work to suit himself, and has no-one telling him what to do. But he has to make sure that his work is always of high quality: if it isn't it won't sell and he won't be able to pay the bills. When he is working he doesn't mind being on his own – other people

18 Work roles change with increasing and changing skill

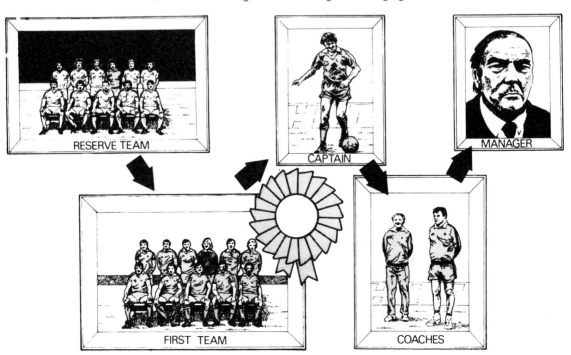

RESERVE TEAM

CAPTAIN

MANAGER

FIRST TEAM

COACHES

might distract him – but it can be lonely when he is clearing up at the end of the day. Moreover, since he is self-employed the National Insurance contributions which he makes would not entitle him to Unemployment Benefit if his business failed. And he earns no money if he is unable to work because of illness.

A 'Girl Friday'

Mary is the 'Girl Friday' for a fast-growing record company. She never stops work from the minute she arrives until everyone else has gone home (whenever that is): she often works until late in the evening. She does all sorts of work – as a receptionist, tea maker, telephonist, typist, pianist, model, signwriter, nurse – and loves every minute of it. Because she feels part of the firm and involved in what she is trying to do, she doesn't mind working very hard. She is quite well paid and sometimes gets to meet famous pop-stars and to go on trips to exciting places as part of the job.

Training Scheme Workers

When David and Myra left school, they knew there was not much chance of a job locally. Most of the big local employers did not need new young workers, especially ones with no qualifications – at least no paper ones. But the Careers Officer who came to see them at school thought they might find something they would like in a training scheme, one of the ones run by the government and local employers. It would give them work experience – in a real job – and training off the job, perhaps in a college. David and Myra spent a long time reading over the lists of possible training places. David was interested in the 'Help' project being run by the local council: painting, decorating and joinery were the skills he could concentrate on. Myra though she would like to try a course linked with a large drugs company. This would give her some experience in laboratory work and perhaps clerical work too. Myra and David were pleased to learn that the off-the-job training at the local college would mean they could meet up with other old school friends on similar training schemes with other companies.

The most important thing about the training scheme was the valuable experience of work it would give: something future employers would be very interested in! There was even a possibility that they would end up with a permanent job with their training scheme employers.

An Assembly-line Worker

Janet answered an advertisement in the local paper for a job on the assembly line in an engineering works. She was attracted by the high pay which was offered and by the opportunities to work overtime, as the shift system had been abandoned.

Her part in the production process is to attach a part to each engine that passes her and tighten a few nuts. At first she found it quite difficult to do the job quickly enough so that the line was not held up. But now the work comes automatically to her and she can let her mind wander to other things while her hands do the work almost by themselves. She can think about lunchtime when she will meet her friends in the subsidised canteen or about her Saturday swim in the new recreation complex which the company built. Any doubts about the monotony of the work were removed when she heard a rumour that the management were planning to retrain most of the semi-skilled workers to do different tasks if the unions could reach agreement on demarcation lines. Her only worry is the threat of redundancy if the orders tail off, but then she would be entitled to enough Benefits to tide her over a bad spell.

A Rig Worker

Jim is a roustabout (general labourer) on a drilling rig in the North Sea. His job is to unload material from the supply boats, but often he is moved up to the drilling deck to help the rough-necks change the drilling bits and fit in new lengths of piping as the drill works deeper. This needs strength, real skill and split-second timing, and on the rigs you learn on the job. Jim can't refuse the American tool-pusher's instructions to take over from an injured roughneck – it is more than his job is worth and he wants to move on to be a driller, watching the seabed on a television screen.

Accidents are common and, as Jim knows a bit of first aid, he is called on to help the injured until the helicopter arrives from Aberdeen, an hour and a half's journey. Worse than injury, however, is the danger of being washed overboard by the huge waves. In winter the cold of the sea kills you instantly; in the summer it numbs your legs in seven minutes.

Jim finds it a strain not being able to smoke during the twelve-hour shift, and it is hard not to be allowed indoors except for the half-way meal break. But at least the food the Spanish cooks prepare is good.

19 Changing a rock bit on a drilling platform east of Shetland

Off-duty time is spent in a four-berth room, with a shower, or in the recreation room where films are shown. No alcohol is allowed. All the workers look forward to their two weeks ashore after two weeks' work, if they can get off the rig. Jim remembers with horror the time his crew had to work for six weeks instead of two because the weather was too bad for the relief crew to be landed.

Jim usually goes home to his family in Edinburgh. Other workers prefer to stay in Aberdeen in boarding houses where they very quickly spend their wages. Perhaps the high wages make up for being away from home and working in such unpleasant conditions.

Questions

1. What are the main reasons for working?
2. List some of the things you would take into account when choosing a job.
3. Describe a football team as if it were a factory, from the unskilled workers to the manager. Include items produced.
4. What are some of the advantages and disadvantages that the potter found in self-employment?
5. What reasons might the assembly-line worker and the rig worker have had for choosing the jobs they did?
6. If you were employed as a Girl Friday, would you feel that you were being exploited? Why?

20 How much is a job worth? Nurse £? Pop Star £?

Work and the Law

Government laws protect the rights of workers and employers in a variety of ways. Workers in jobs which are not covered by a strong trade union or similar organisation are particularly in need of this protection. All workers must have a written contract detailing hours of work, pay, holidays, disciplinary rules and how to complain. There also has to be information on how much notice must be given by a worker who leaves and the rules which operate should a worker be made redundant. In most cases a worker has protection against unfair dismissal and can take a complaint about this to an Industrial Tribunal.

21 A contract of employment

CONTRACT OF EMPLOYMENT

FIXED TERM CONTRACT

Employee to be given top copy - Employer to retain duplicate.

This form is designed to assist employers in meeting the requirements of the Employment Protection (Consolidation) Act, 1979 and the Employment Act, 1980

This statement dated.................... sets out the main particulars of the terms and conditions of
which: (NAME OF EMPLOYER)...
employs (NAME OF EMPLOYEE)...
Your employment began on ....and the employment with your previous employer does not count as part of your continuous period of employment.

PART I - MAIN TERMS AND CONDITIONS

TITLE OF JOB	You are employed as
PAY	Your salary/wage will be paid at...............intervals by cash/cheque/banker's order Details:
NORMAL HOURS OF WORK	Your normal hours are: Other terms and conditions:
HOLIDAY ENTITLEMENT AND PAY	(if none, say so)
SICKNESS OR INJURY	Details of terms and conditions and any sick pay benefits (if none, say so)
PENSIONS AND PENSION SCHEMES	Schemes in operation (if none, say so)
RIGHTS TO NOTICE TERMINATION OF EMPLOYMENT	Notice to be given by employer: Notice to be given by employees: ....(weeks) .... (weeks) By mutual agreement these notices can be waived by either party. Payment in lieu of notice may be accepted. In addition the first..........weeks of the employment are a probationary period and the employer or employee may, without notice discontinue the employment upon the expiry of the probationary period.
EXPIRY OF TERM	This contract is for a fixed term. The date of expiry is.............................

PART II - ADDITIONAL NOTE

DISCIPLINARY RULES	State any disciplinary rules applicable to the employee, if any (or refer to any document that contains any disciplinary rules).
	If you are dissatisfied with any disciplinary decision you should raise it orally/in writing with:
GRIEVANCE PROCEDURE	If you have any grievance relating to your employment you should raise it orally/in writing with:
SOCIAL SECURITY PENSIONS	A contracting out certificate is/is not in force for the employment in respect of which this statement is given.
TRADE UNION MEMBERSHIP	You may join a Trade Union should you so wish, but you are not obliged to.
	Any changes of terms mentioned above will be notified within one month, and the office record is available for inspection.

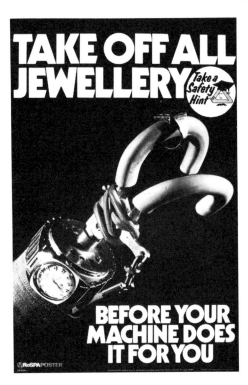

22 Health and Safety at Work poster

By the Health and Safety Act (1974 and 1978), committees of workers or representatives can check safety precautions, lighting and heating, and have changes made should it appear that the law has been broken.

Women's rights are covered by a number of laws: for example, the Equal Pay Act (1970), Sex Discrimination Act (1975) and Employment Protection Act (1975). Women cannot be sacked because of pregnancy; they must be allowed time off for antenatal care; they must receive maternity pay and have the right, with certain conditions, to return to work after the birth. Women are not allowed to work in certain very dangerous jobs and are not normally allowed to work long hours.

By law, men and women doing broadly similar work should receive the same pay, and a woman should get the same opportunity to apply for, work and be promoted in a job as a man.

By the Race Relations Act (1976), employers cannot choose not to employ a worker on the grounds of their sex, religion, colour or race. Nor can the employer operate a recruitment scheme which discriminates against black workers: for example, by adding a question to an application form which puts black workers at a disadvantage, or by only employing people from white areas.

TRIBUNALS

The fact that these laws exist does not mean that they are always upheld or enforced. Workers who feel they have been unfairly treated, for example discriminated against or sacked unfairly, can take their case to a Tribunal. It is the Tribunal's job to hear both the worker's and the employer's cases and decide whether the law has been broken. Tribunals give the workers added protection and more chance to ensure that the law is kept. However, in many cases (particularly with discrimination), it is very difficult to prove that the law has been broken.

CASE STUDY:

The Industrial Tribunal

Helen worked as a manageress in a large restaurant in a busy shopping centre. She was quite happy at her work until she discovered that the manager of another restaurant owned by the same firm was paid more money for doing what she thought was the same job. She became angry when she realised that many of the waitresses who worked under her were taking home more money than she was, because of the tips they received.

Helen contacted her union and was advised to put her case to her employers and see if she could be given the same wage as the manager she had heard about. She asked for, and was granted, an interview, but it didn't last long. 'You're a woman,' they said, 'you can't manage the waitresses as well as a man. And besides, what if you marry and start a family? You'll leave us and we'll need to train someone else.'

Helen went straight from that interview to the Employment Office to complain. They gave her an application form for an appeal to the Industrial Tribunal.

At the hearing, Helen pointed out that she did the same work as the other manager, that she had worked for the firm longer than he had, and that the Equal Pay Act entitled her to the same wages. After asking the owners of the chain of restaurants some questions, the three men on the Tribunal discussed the case briefly before giving their verdict. The member from the trade unionist panel was in no doubt. 'Exploitation of women – time it was stopped,' he said. The employer member wanted to ask some questions about the waitresses but was advised that this was not relevant in this case, since it only had to be decided whether Helen was doing broadly similar work to that of the man. The chairman, who was a lawyer, didn't even have to ask for a vote. They were unanimous in their agreement that the restaurant owners would have to pay Helen the same wages as the other manager.

The chairman was glad that this case was so straightforward: some of those he had to deal with concerning the Sex Discrimination Act, or the Employment Protection Act, among others, could be very complicated, especially if the other two on the tribunal disagreed and he had to decide with his casting vote.

Questions

1. What protection does a written contract give both the worker and the employer?
2. What legal protection is given to the following people? A new worker, a worker threatened with redundancy, women, black workers, all workers.
3. Describe some of the problems that might occur at work if the government did not protect workers through laws.
4. If a worker was unfairly dismissed, describe what steps they could take to protect themselves.

Pay
TYPES OF PAY

The basic pay which people receive, before any extras or deductions, can be calculated in two ways: according to what they produce (piece rate: the more they produce the more they are paid); or according to the amount of time they work (time rate: this can be hourly, weekly or monthly).

There are various extras, increases or bonuses that a worker can earn or be entitled to, depending on the job they have.

● *Increments* are fixed increases paid for each year of service. They encourage workers to stay with one firm, or to stay in one job. There are usually a limited number of increments (say, six yearly steps) before a worker reaches the full rate for the job. For example, young workers might get an increment each year until they reach adult wage; teachers get an increment each year until they reach maximum pay.

● *Commission* is a bonus paid for making a sale. Often the basic pay is low and workers can increase their take-home pay by working harder to make more sales and so earn more commission. Car sales people and shop assistants often work on a commission basis.

● *Overtime* is $1\frac{1}{2}$ or 2 times the usual rate of pay and is paid to workers who work outside their normal working hours, for example on Sundays.

● *Productivity bonuses* are paid to workers who agree to change their way of working, perhaps by using a new machine, to increase the amount they produce. When a government incomes policy imposes restrictions on pay increases, this is one of the few acceptable forms of wage increase, because it is not inflationary.

● *Promotion* usually means a fairly large wage increase because it involves moving to a more skilled job or a job in which there is more responsibility (e.g. a manager in charge of other people).

● *Merit payments* cover a wide range of bonuses: from rewards for good time-keeping to rewards for high-quality work.

● *Fringe benefits* include company cars, cheap mortgages, clothing allowances, discounts on company products, membership of private health schemes, free **insurance** and luncheon vouchers. They can mean quite a lot to the worker: a car is 'worth' about £2000 a year, although the worker has to pay tax on it. Fringe benefits are not usually affected by a government incomes policy.

GETTING A RISE

Pay rises come in many forms: a flat rate (lump sum), a percentage increase, a cost of living rise, bonus payments and fringe benefits.

More Money for Tom and Paula

Tom, a machine operator, and Paula, a manager, both work for the same firm and have been offered a variety of types of wage increase in this year's pay rise.

last year both accepted a flat rate increase of £500. This brought Tom's wage up to £6000 and Paula's up to £20 000. Paula found that £20 000 was not a lot more than £19 500, but the extra £500 made quite a bit of difference to Tom.

This year the firm has offered a 'package deal' of a percentage increase plus a number of bonuses and benefits. Tom will gain £600 from the 10% increase, but Paula will gain £2000: a lot more. Because Tom is a low-paid worker, and has a large family, he had been able to claim Family Income Supplement until he got this rise. Now he is too highly paid to qualify for this or other Benefits, such as free school meals. He thinks he is worse off than he was before the rise if the loss of welfare benefits is taken into account. (This is called the 'poverty trap'.) Paula says that most of her increase will go in tax.

The 'package deal' includes a cost of living rise: every time the Retail Price Index shows that the cost of living has risen more than 1% the workers will automatically receive a 1% increase in pay.

Tom has been offered a bonus if he agrees to use a new machine which will enable him to make more of the radio parts he welds together. This will be a productivity bonus since it will allow Tom to produce more parts in the same time. Paula has also been offered more money – an increment – because she has worked for the firm for another year (her third) and the firm benefits from her experience.

Both Tom and Paula get fringe benefits. Tom gets luncheon vouchers, free overalls and cheap travel to the factory in the works bus. Paula gets a company car, a cheap mortgage and discount on any company product that she wants to buy.

23 What a typical pay slip means

- *Tax Code* Given to worker by Inland Revenue to enable tax to be deducted correctly. The number gives information on tax-free allowances due. The letter indicates marital status, i.e. married or single (L means single: lower allowances).
- *Basic pay* Wages before any additions or deductions have been made.
- *Overtime* Extra money for working outside normal hours.
- *Bonus* Extra money for time-keeping, productivity, etc.
- *Gross pay* Basic pay plus all additions.
- *Superann.* Superannuation: usually a percentage of basic pay to pension fund.
- *Dues* Trade union dues and contributions: may be paid directly by firm to union on member's behalf.
- *Nat. Ins.* National Insurance contributions: earnings related, a percentage of earnings if the earner is an employee.
- *Savings* Money deducted by employer to be paid into special savings scheme, e.g. holiday fund, Christmas club.
- *Net pay* Wages after all deductions have been made: what you get 'in your hand'.

INCOME TAX

Everyone who earns money is liable to pay income tax. In order to work out how much, a calculation is first made of how much income is to be exempt from tax (allowances). This depends on whether the income earner is single or married, has dependent relatives or other expenses. The remainder of the income is taxed at so much in the pound, but any income beyond a certain sum is taxed at a higher rate. Both the allowances and tax rates are fixed by the Chancellor of the Exchequer in the Budget.

Most people pay the tax due by Pay As You Earn (PAYE). The income earner fills in a tax form which enables an Inspector of Taxes to calculate how much tax the earner should pay in a tax year (6 April to 5 April); the tax office supplies the employer with the appropriate tax code for the employee; and the employer then deducts the tax directly from the employee's wage and pays it to the Inland Revenue.

Income tax, along with taxes on capital (e.g. Capital Transfer Tax on money left after a person dies, and Capital Gains Tax on money made buying and selling shares or property) and taxes on expenditure (VAT), is added to money that the government has borrowed and National Insurance contributions. With this money the government is able to pay for roads, law and order, housing, the arts, defence, overseas aid, interest payments on the National Debt, etc.

Questions

1. Name some ways that workers can increase their basic pay.
2. Who should be paid more: a pop singer or a nurse? Why?
3. Describe the advantages of (a) a flat rate rise, (b) a percentage rise, (c) a productivity bonus, (d) a fringe benefit.
4. What are the main deductions from gross pay?
5. What reasons are there for some workers being paid more than others?
6. How does the government use the money raised through income tax?

Name	Tax code	Basic pay	Bonus	Overtime	Gross pay	Tax	Superann.	Union dues	Nat. Ins.	Savings	Net pay
YOUNG, F.	178L										
National Ins. No.		140.00	15.00	25.00	180.00	53.00	9.00	0.50	7.00	10.00	100.50
AB112345A											

3. Buying and Selling

Budgeting

MONEY AND THE MARSHALLS

Margaret Marshall and her mother are looking through travel brochures. Margaret wants to go abroad for their summer holiday but her mother is not so sure.

Dad: (*coming into room*) Starting a travel agent's are we?

Margaret: Look at this swimming pool, Dad, and the disco, the beach. The price is only . . .

Dad: £350 each! Do you think I'm made of money!

Margaret: But if we go in May it's cheaper and think of the sun!

Mum: It does look nice. Couldn't we use the money we have in the bank, and there's your rise . . .

Dad: You've started to pack already! Let's write down how much it will cost us, and how much money we'll have by May.

```
2 adults at £350      700
1 adult  at £350      350 (Margaret)
1 child  at £200      200 (Jimmy)
                     ————
                     1250

Money in bank    600
Likely rise      300 (20 weeks at £15)
                ————
                 900
```

Dad: We'll never do it! We're short of £350 and that doesn't count spending money and clothes!

Mum: But there must be lots of things we can do to save money. Let's make a list of how much we spend every month, and see if we can cut down on anything.

```
rent             80
rates            45
electricity      30
hire purchase    40
food            120
travel           35
pocket money     30
clothing         70
                ————
                450
```

Dad: I work out that we have about £20 left at the end of each month. We have to pay rent and rates, electricity, and hire purchase. Can we cut the rest a bit? Do without a few luxuries like sweets and expensive clothes? Maybe walk to work? I think I like the idea of two weeks lazing in the sun!

It didn't take the Marshalls long to see where they could cut back. They had to pay some bills: the ones for the house for example, but many of the others could be reduced or cut out completely.

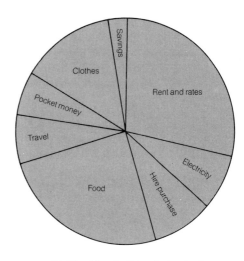

24 The Marshall family budget

SAVING

Some people save money in a jam jar, but this is not very wise. Not only might it be stolen but, after a year, £100 kept in a jam jar is still £100, that is if it hasn't already been spent. If savings are invested they can earn **interest**. For example, if the interest rate is 5%, £100 becomes £105 by the end of the year. There are many ways money can be saved or invested.

● *Banks*, such as the Bank of Scotland, Midland Bank, Trustee Savings Bank, offer a variety of different types of account. The two most common are: (a) a current account, which does not earn interest (National Giro operates like this) but enables you to pay bills with a cheque or by standing order (when the bank arranges regular payments such as the mortgage and television rental for you); (b) a deposit account, which earns interest (but tax must be paid on this). Some banks have other services: cheque cards, credit cards, cash cards, **loans**. Some have special rules for withdrawals (e.g. a month's notice).

● *Save As You Earn* is a way of saving a fixed amount each month through the Department for National Savings. At the end of five years you get your money back plus interest calculated on the rate of inflation each month. Your savings are 'index-linked' and therefore 'inflation proof'.

● *Stocks and shares* can be bought through a broker on the Stock Exchange. This is a way of lending a company money to help them expand their business, for which you receive a dividend (a share of the company's profits). If the company is very successful you could make a lot of money. If, however, the company loses money you may lose yours.

● *Unit Trusts* are run by people who invest investors' money in the shares of many different companies. This means the risk involved in buying shares is spread over many companies. Usually the value of unit trusts goes up when the companies are prospering, but, if there is a general slump, unit trusts suffer.

● *Life Insurance* involves paying a sum of money (premium) each month to an insurance company, and in return you (or your dependants) will receive a fixed sum (the amount saved plus interest) at an agreed age.

● *Building Societies* have many different savings schemes: some are like bank deposit accounts; others offer a higher interest rate in return for restrictions on withdrawing money, or a large initial deposit. Interest is paid with income tax already deducted. Building Societies use the money deposited with them to lend people large sums of money, on mortgage, to buy a house.

Questions

1. Make a list of the ways the Marshall family could save enough money to go on holiday.
2. Which method of saving would you choose for each of the following, and why? (a) Your weekly spending money, (b) £1000 left to you by an aunt (c) £30 a month which you do not normally spend out of your pay, (d) money to pay bills, (e) money being saved for an expensive item such as a car, (f) money for retirement.

Shops

The most important change in shops in recent years has been the growth of large multiple retailers (superstores) such as Tesco and Asda which sell a very wide range of products. These shops enable people to buy their weekly (or even monthly) shopping in one place, and are especially convenient for people who have very little free time and have cars. Small independent shops often find that they lose customers to the supermarkets and superstores, which can usually offer lower prices as well as convenience. These large stores are able to sell standard goods at lower prices because they buy container loads of items direct from the suppliers rather than smaller quantities from wholesalers. They also sell 'own-brand' lines at very competitive prices. New purpose-built shopping centres, like the one in Milton Keynes, are very successful in attracting customers from a wide area, again because they offer the convenience of a complete range of goods in one place.

25 A local high street: 1950s and 1980s

Baker	Grocer	Dairy	Newsagent	Hardware	Cafe	Greengrocer	Bank	Tailor/ Outfitters	Fish shop	Baby clothes & haberdashery	Chemist	Post Office	Flower shop	Clothes shop	Butcher

Supermarket	Chain newsagent	Bakery/ Take away	Building Society	Estate Agent	Bank	Fashion store	Chain fruit & veg. shop	Chain chemist	Post Office	Video & records	Travel Agent

Questions

1. Look at the shops table. What would be the best type of shop to go to for each of the following purchases? (Give a reason for each answer.) (a) A loaf of bread at 9 p.m., (b) an old-age pensioner's weekly groceries, (c) the weekly groceries for a large family, (d) a new suit for a farmer living on a remote croft, (e) a new washing machine.

2. Describe the changes that have taken place in the types of shops since the 1950s.

26 Milton Keynes shopping centre

27 Shops

Type of shop	Advantages	Disadvantages
Small family business	Personal service; nearby; often open late	Often expensive; service may be slow; limited range of goods
Volume chain of small businesses, e.g. Spar, Mace	Personal service; nearby; many own brands; some special offers because of bulk buying	Some items may be expensive; limited range of goods
Multiple stores, e.g. Saxone	Cheap; high standards; own brands	High Street only; lack of variety
Department stores, e.g. Frasers, John Lewis, Selfridges	One-stop for everything; luxurious	Often expensive; parking often difficult in town centre
Self-service supermarkets e.g. Safeway, Waitrose	Self-selection; low prices; loss leaders; wide choice; own brands	Checkout queues; wide range encourages impulse buying; impersonal
Hypermarkets and superstores, e.g. Asda	Self-selection; one-stop; low prices; own brands; parking; wide range of goods	Remote edge-of-town site: car needed
Cut-price discount stores, e.g. Horizon, MFI	Low prices, parking	Limited range; limited aftersales service
Door-to-door and personal service e.g. Avon	Convenient, no effort	Under pressure from sales people
Mail order catalogues, e.g. Grattan, Kays	Convenient, buy at leisure	Danger of impulse buying; cannot see goods

Advertising

Advertising is the main method by which **consumers** are persuaded to buy a particular brand of something. It might be a necessity, a luxury, or indeed a type of saving.

The producers want to tell consumers of the existence of their product and to emphasise some new or special quality in their brand. They also want to encourage brand loyalty: to make people ask for their brand by name (e.g. 'McPherson's Brown' rather than 'a brown loaf').

There have been criticisms of advertising on many grounds:

- the consumer pays for advertising in the end through higher prices;
- the consumer can be misled through exaggerated claims or relatively little information;
- consumers may be persuaded to buy things they don't really need or want;
- our language is spoiled by silly slogans, invented words and changed meanings;
- some advertisements are offensive to certain groups of people.

The advertising agencies would reply that:

- they give useful information to help consumers choose wisely;
- competition between producers, and increased sales, keep prices down;
- adverts brighten up the media and help reduce the cost of independent broadcasting, newspapers and magazines;
- advertising is an essential part of a free democratic society.

PLANNING AN ADVERTISING CAMPAIGN

Where there is no great difference between brands of the same product, an advertising agency must try to come up with a campaign to persuade consumers that their client's brand is better in some ways than its rivals. This applies particularly to products such as washing powders, toothpaste and cigarettes, where consumer preference is often a matter of habit.

When a new brand of a product is launched, a lot of research is done to find out who is likely to buy it. Then a number of possible names and packagings are tried to see which appeals most to customers. Different ways of promoting and advertising the brand are discussed until the company chooses the one it thinks will be the most successful with the public. For example, a new washing powder, called 'Cleano', packaged in white and yellow might be advertised as getting clothes as clean and bright as a sunny day.

Once the main theme of the campaign is decided, the details have to be worked out. The selling technique of the advert has to be chosen, and this might be used for magazine, newspaper and poster campaigns, as well as television and radio commercials. An expert or celebrity might be paid to promote the product, saying how outstanding it is; or there might be scientific evidence presented to show the shining whiteness of the wash;. or happy families might be shown, to suggest that Cleano helps to bring such happiness! Other techniques (not appropriate for advertising washing powder) can be used: for example, adverts for perfume or clothes might suggest that they increase popularity,

28 A modern advert using a celebrity to promote the product

give the wearer a new image or make friends envious; some adverts are designed to remind people of the good old days when things were natural and wholesome. The advertiser hopes that if people like the advert, the catchy tune accompanying the commercial or the eyecatching packaging, they will be persuaded to buy this brand rather than any other.

An important concern for advertisers is the potential buyers and their reading and television watching habits. Market research by advertisers shows that most washing powder is bought by women, so adverts for this will go in women's magazines and at times when research shows many women watch television. Cars are advertised in newspapers, colour supplements of Sunday papers and during breaks in sports or 'men's' programmes, because advertisers believe most car buyers are men. The choice of newspaper is important too. Surveys have shown that better-off people tend to read quality newspapers, and that less-well-off people tend to read the popular press. Therefore expensive goods, such as diamond jewellery, paintings, and high-price cars, will appear in the quality press. Supermarket adverts, and those for cheaper cars, are more likely to appear in the popular press: the papers the advertisers think their customers read.

As added incentives to buy, special offers and free gifts often accompany the launch of a new brand. Discount vouchers and free samples are often brought out at the same time as the introductory television adverts. Later there might be competitions or special offers that involve collecting labels. These are designed to build up customer loyalty to that particular brand. The shopkeepers are also encouraged to stock up with the new brand: the company sales representatives will have special gifts and competitions for them too.

CONTROL OF ADVERTISING

About £2880 million was spent on advertising of all sorts in 1981. This was almost 2% of the gross national product (see page 50). There are laws and codes of conduct to regulate advertising and prevent consumers being misled.

Laws such as the Trade Descriptions Act protect the buyer from misleading advertising. Codes such as that of the Advertising Standards Authority (the advertisers themselves) aim to make all adverts 'legal, clean, honest and truthful'. This means that adverts must not break an exisiting law, offend public decency or morality, or tells lies about their own or rival products.

Television prohibits some types of advertising: for example, for cigarettes, betting, political or religious groups. Certain techniques are also banned: for example, subliminal advertising, in which the name of the product is momentarily flashed on the screen and only subconsciously seen by the viewer. Famous personalities must not be used to advertise products directed at children. Advertising time is limited to seven minutes per hour for television and nine minutes for radio. Adverts have to be obviously separate from the programme and are not allowed at all between certain types of programme, e.g. schools' broadcasts.

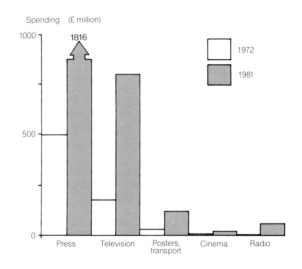

29 Money spent on advertising
(Source: Advertising Association)

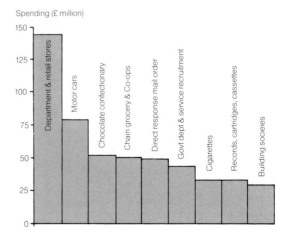

30 The big spenders in advertising
(Source: Media Expenditure Analysis)

Cinema advertising is covered by a broadly similar code but here adverts must be vetted by the British Board of Film Censors and receive similar certificates (U, 15, PG, 18) to those given to films.

Posters also have to meet certain standards, and the siting of the billboards is controlled by the local authority planning department.

The Advertising Standards Authority (ASA) was set up by the advertising industry to keep a check on published advertisements. It makes sure that advertisements keep to the British Code of Advertising practice, and judges whether complaints from the public are justified or not. It is funded by a levy of 0.1% on the cost of advertising in the areas it deals with: the press, posters, print and cinema.

The ASA checks adverts in a sample of editions of newspapers. For example on average, national daily papers are examined every fourth issue. Adverts for twelve product categories, those most often complained about, are examined. Since 1981, random checks have been made and advertisers asked to prove the claims made in their adverts.

The ASA staff has been criticised for not preventing the use of adverts which might give offence to sections of the community. Some people feel that an independent body is needed to monitor the advertising industry.

Questions

1. What are the main reasons for advertising?
2. What are the main criticisms of advertising methods?
3. Describe the methods used to persuade consumers to buy.
4. Write a slogan that would be illegal for a new powder for helping to relieve cold symptoms. Explain why it would be illegal.
5. Work out an advertising campaign for one of the following: a new washing powder; oranges; a luxury car.
6. Why and how does the Advertising Standards Authority check adverts?
7. Is the money spent on advertising justified? Give a reason for your answer.

Consumers' Rights

Until the 1960s and 1970s, consumers' demands were not taken seriously enough. Most laws, apart from the 1893 Sale of Goods Act, protected the rights of businesses rather than those of the shopper. Since then, however, many laws and other forms of protection have been introduced which have attempted to redress the balance.

● 1957 *Consumers' Association* was set up; and brought out *Which?* magazine.
● 1961 *Consumer Protection Act* outlawed dangerous products, such as inflammable nightclothes and unsafe electrical items.
● 1963 *Weights and Measures Act:* the weight or quantity of goods had to be marked or made known at the time of purchase.
● 1968 *Trade Descriptions Act* made it illegal to describe inaccurately the goods or services offered. A hotel described as having a swimming pool must have one! Sale goods must have genuine price reductions.
● 1971 *Unsolicited Goods and Services Act* made it an offence to demand payment for goods not ordered; for example, sent through the post by mistake.
● 1973 *Office of Fair Trading* set up to investigate unfair trading practices; it established codes of practice and complaints procedures.
● 1973 *Supply of Goods (Implied terms) Act* came into force. With this law behind them, people could take a trader who had done a bad piece of work or sold faulty goods to court without fear of enormous costs. It curbed the use of small-print get-out clauses.
● 1974 *Consumer Credit Act* controlled the activities of creditors, brokers, owners of hired equipment, debt collectors, etc. Lending organisations had to be licensed by the Director General of Fair Trading. Later additions to this Act forced traders to show the true cost of paying on credit terms (i.e. paying in instalments over a number of months or years).
● 1977 *Unfair Contract Terms Act* tightened up the law on get-out clauses.
● 1978 *Consumer Safety Act* gave wider powers to deal with unsafe products.
● 1982 *Supply of Goods and Services Act* (not Scotland) made it easier to claim rights when making a complaint.

Many people learn about their shopping rights from special columns in newspapers and magazines or from television consumer programmes. The National Consumer Council is an independent organisation which ensures that consumers' views are made known to government and industries. Citizen's Advice Bureaux (or Consumer Advice Centres) provide information and advice about shopping problems for the general public. There are also Consumer Councils for nationalised industries supplying the consumer, such as gas, electricity and railways, who investigate problems that customers have.

This case study shows how one man was helped with a shopping problem by his local Citizen's Advice Centre.

Questions

1. With which laws and in what ways does the government protect the consumer if (a) a fishmonger's scales are weighing incorrectly, (b) a toy is dangerous to a young child, (c) un-ordered records are received through the post, (d) a hotel described in the brochure as 'on the beach' is ten minutes' walk from it, (e) a pair of shoes fall apart on their first wearing.
2. Describe the steps you should take when faced with a shopping problem.

NO REFUNDS?

Noel Barton bought some new clothes in the winter sales. He was delighted with his purchases, until he took them home. He hadn't noticed the strange coloured blotches on the back of the sweater before, and the shirt fitted but it didn't match anything else in his wardrobe. Noel was quite angry. His 'bargains' were a waste of money if he couldn't wear them, but he couldn't take them back because there had been a notice in the shop saying 'No refunds on sale goods'.

That night he told his story to some friends. Most of them were full of sympathy and said, 'Hard Luck!' and 'Sales are like that!' But one friend thought Noel could do something. She wrote down the telephone number of the local Citizen's Advice Bureau and told Noel to phone them.

The Citizen's Advice Bureau staff were not surprised to hear of Noel's problems. A lot of people thought they could not get their money back if they bought something in a sale. But, in fact, the 'No refunds' sign was illegal.

Armed with this information, Noel went back to the shop and politely asked to speak to the manager. To begin with, the manager just pointed to the sign, then she realised Noel knew something about consumers' rights. As the Citizen's Advice Bureau had said, Noel was given a refund for the faulty sweater. The shop were not legally obliged to do anything about the shirt – it wasn't their fault that the shirt didn't match Noel's clothes – but to show their goodwill they offered to exchange it for other goods of the same value.

4. The Welfare State

Background

ORIGINS AND AIMS

At one time, people in Britain were expected to look after themselves, even if they suffered a misfortune that was not their fault and if others dependent on them suffered as well. For example, a married couple with a large family might have an invalid parent to support, but only have one wage coming into the house. They might have the same income as a single person with no dependants but would have many more bills to pay and would therefore be struggling to manage.

There were some voluntary organisations and charities, and some government measures, to help people in difficult circumstances but it was felt that these were not enough and that the government, or State, ought to do more. Remembering the depression of the 1920s and 1930s, and looking forward to a better society when the war was over, the wartime coalition government set up the Beveridge Committee in 1941 to see what could be done. This Committee first of all identified five main areas of need which ought to be remedied.

● *Poverty*. Many people did not have enough money to buy the necessities of life such as food, clothing and shelter.

● *Disease*. Medicine was advancing rapidly but many people did not know how to keep themselves healthy, nor could they afford treatment when they became ill or disabled, because it was costly.

● *Ignorance*. Many children grew up without a proper education because their parents could not afford to send them to, or keep them at, school.

● *Squalor*. The living conditions, especially the houses, in which many people lived, were cramped, dirty and lacking in basic amenities.

● *Idleness*. A lack of suitable jobs meant that many people were unemployed, and they and their dependants did not have a decent income.

The Beveridge Committee said that if all British citizens were to be safe from such suffering, the State would have to look after their welfare, so they recommended the setting up of a Welfare State which should be:

(a) *universal*, i.e. everyone should be eligible for the benefits provided, regardless of income or other conditions;

(b) *comprehensive*, i.e. all likely areas of need should be catered for;

(c) *adequate*, i.e. the benefits and services should be enough to provide a minimum standard of living, a 'safety net';

(d) *normal*, i.e. benefits should be provided as a basic right, not as an act of charity.

By 1948, the post-war Labour Government had passed the necessary legislation to set up the Welfare State. Successive Governments altered the system to improve the benefits and include other deserving cases as their needs became known. We now have a complex system of State Benefits, allowances and services which are often said to cover an individual 'from the cradle to the grave'.

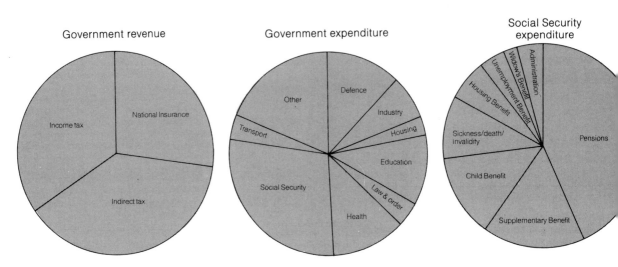

31 Finance in the Welfare State

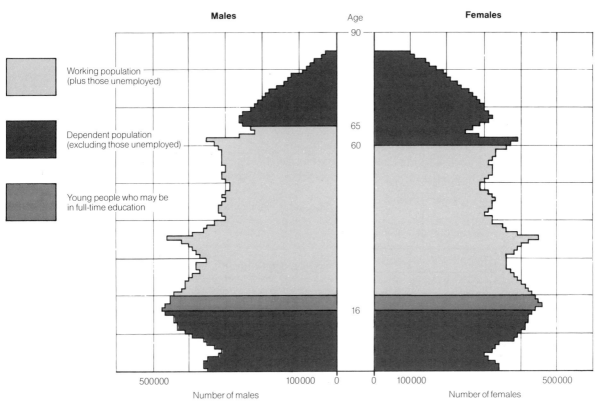

Males   Age   **Females**

Working population
(plus those unemployed)

Dependent population
(excluding those unemployed)

Young people who may be
in full-time education

90

65
60

16

500000   100000   0   0   100000   500000

Number of males   Number of females

32 The population graph for Great Britain in the 1980s

PAYING FOR THE WELFARE STATE

The money used to pay for the Welfare State comes from two main sources: National Insurance contributions and **taxation**. National Insurance contributions are paid by all working people (self-employed and employed). In the case of an employee, the contribution is paid partly by the employee, partly by the employer and partly by the government. As the number of people in work is only a small proportion of the total number of people in the country, the National Insurance fund is not enough on its own to pay for the Welfare State, and needs to be topped up by money from taxation.

In 1964 around 350 000 people were unemployed. By 1984 this figure had increased tenfold to 3.5 million. So the number of people depending on the Welfare State has risen. National Health Service treatments have become more sophisticated and more expensive. People live longer, so there are more old people needing medical care and financial help. These and other rising costs mean that a larger share of government money is needed to pay for the Welfare State.

The Conservative Party believes that people should take more responsibility for their own 'welfare'. They encourage private medicine and private housing. They have also tried to cut back Benefit levels, tax some Benefits and reduce the range of Benefits available from the Department of Health and Social Security. Some, such as the Housing Benefit and Clothing Grants, have become the responsibility of local authorities and are paid out of their funds.

The Labour Party has criticised these policies. It thinks the State has a duty to look after those who cannot, for the time being, look after themselves. Its priorities would be to try to create jobs for the unemployed, raise Benefits to a higher level, and cut the private sector.

Questions

1. Why was the Welfare State set up?
2. Where does the money come from to pay for the Welfare State?
3. What is the money spent on?
4. What does Fig. **32** show about the dependence of some people on others?

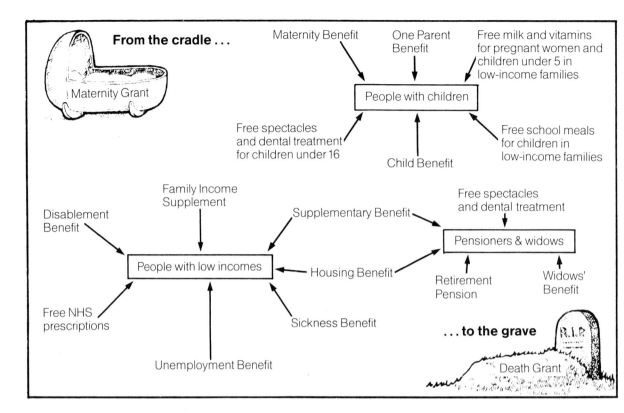

33 The various Benefits available in Britain today

Social Security

A wide range of State Benefits is available. Some Benefits are paid only to people who have contributed (through National Insurance). These include Unemployment, Sickness, and Widows' Benefits, Retirement Pension and Death Grant. The National Insurance Fund pays for these Benefits but has to be topped up from taxation. Other Benefits are non-contributory and are paid out of taxation to people with special needs, regardless of whether they have paid National Insurance contributions or not. Child Benefit and War Pensions are examples. The third type of Benefit is means-tested, also paid out of taxation: for example, Supplementary Benefit and Family Income Supplement. People are entitled to these Benefits if they can show they do not have enough money to meet their needs.

THE POVERTY TRAP

With an increase in pay, a poor family can face a higher tax bill and lose entitlement to some of its Social Security Benefits, often ending up no better off (or even worse off) than before. Major changes in the taxation system would be needed to allow those on low incomes to escape income tax altogether; merely raising the tax-free personal allowances would benefit the rich as well as the poor.

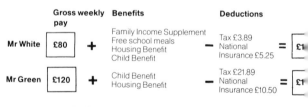

	Gross weekly pay		Benefits	Deductions	
Mr White	£80	+	Family Income Supplement Free school meals Housing Benefit Child Benefit	− Tax £3.89 National Insurance £5.25	= £1
Mr Green	£120	+	Child Benefit Housing Benefit	− Tax £21.89 National Insurance £10.50	= £1

Mr Green has a higher wage than Mr White. He is not therefore entitled to many Benefits and has to pay more tax and higher National Insurance contributions. Because of this, his extra £40 pay is not worth much: he is only £4 or so better off than Mr White once the Benefits have been taken into account.

34 The poverty trap (April 1983)

The Scroungers?

The Social Security system is sometimes criticised because some people are able to claim Benefits that they are not entitled to: for example Unemployment Benefit while working. A special group of workers from the Department of Social Security (DHSS) investigate claimants who might be guilty of abusing the system, and there are widely ranging estimates about the amount of money saved when 'scroungers' are caught. Many people, including some DHSS staff, are unhappy about investigations into supposed scroungers as they feel genuine claimants may be put off asking for Benefits. They also suggest that investigations into people who dodge paying income tax on a large scale would save the government much more money than investigations into those who 'scrounge' a few pounds a week.

UNCLAIMED BENEFITS

As Table **35** shows, a great many people do not apply for the Benefits they are entitled to. Some, especially the old, are too proud to seek help; they look on Social Security as a charity handout. Some people find the forms too difficult to fill in and others do not like to reveal details of their savings (people with more than about £2500 saved cannot receive certain Benefits). The range of Benefits available is so large and the conditions of entitlement change so often that many people find it difficult to discover what Benefits they might be entitled to.

35 Take up of selected Benefits (those 'taking up' Benefit as percentage of those entitled)

Supplementary Benefit (all)	74%
(Pensioners)	65%
Family Income Supplement	50%
Free school meals	12%
Free welfare foods	4%
One parent benefit	70%

(Source: *The Economist* 1 October 1983)

(MORI survey for London Weekend Television programme 'Breadline Britain')

The DHSS has made some improvements in their forms and information booklets. They are more clearly laid out and easier to understand. The counter staff try to explain the range of Benefits available, but are often too overworked to spend a long time with a client. Social workers know a lot about the people they are visiting and can advise on the Benefits they should claim. Particularly in areas where the 'take-up' of benefits is low, the Social Work Departments employ Welfare Rights Officers, and in other areas claimants' unions try to help people who are bewildered by the range of Benefits and the rules applying to each.

THE LOW LEVEL OF BENEFITS

Many pressure groups, such as Age Concern, the Child Poverty Action Group and those for the disabled, claim that Benefits paid are too low. In addition some Benefits are taxed. Poor people tend to spend a larger proportion of their income on food than other people do, and food prices increase faster than other prices used to calculate the inflation rate. Many people argue that Benefits should increase by more than the inflation rate to make up for this difference between the spending pattern of 'Benefit' families and the basket of items used to work out the inflation rate.

Essentials for the 1980s

Two out of three people think these are essential: heating for living areas, indoor toilet, damp-free house, own bath, enough bedrooms, money for public transport, three meals a day, warm coat, fridge, washing machine, toys, Christmas celebration. More than one in two think a television is essential.

But
3 million people live in homes they can't afford to heat;
4 million people live in damp homes;
6 million people are in arrears with essential bills for the last year;
7 million people haven't enough money to pay for the food they need;
more than 3 million people have to buy second-hand clothes.

Questions

1. What is the difference between a contributory and a non-contributory Benefit? Give an example of each.
2. Why can it be difficult for a poor family to get out of the 'poverty trap'?
3. (a) How might a DHSS worker whose job it is to investigate claimants feel about 'scroungers'?
   (b) How might a person who was claiming a Benefit they are not entitled to defend themselves?
4. Why do many people not apply for Benefits they are entitled to?
5. What can be done to increase the uptake of Benefits?
6. Why is there still poverty in the Welfare State?

The National Health Service

The National Health Service (NHS) provides a comprehensive range of medical services, including hospitals, General Practitioners, district nursing services, dentists, opticians and chiropodists. National Insurance contributions go towards paying for the NHS but an increasing amount of money from taxation is needed to meet the rising costs of paying for the nation's health care. There are charges for some parts of the service, for prescriptions and spectacles for example, but many groups of people get all medical services free of charge.

One of the big successes of the NHS is preventative medicine. Diseases such as diptheria, polio, whooping cough and measles are rare now because of innoculation programmes. Increased life expectancy is another sign of better general health.

THE COST OF THE NHS

As Table 36 shows, the NHS costs a great deal of money, and the signs are that this cost will rise.

The most up-to-date treatments for illnesses often need complicated costly operations with expensive modern equipment, drugs and sometimes a long time in intensive care. Highly skilled technicians as well as medical staff are needed in large numbers. People today expect a high standard of medical care and treatment for a range of illnesses. It would not be possible to stop this or cut it back. This explains the big increase in nursing, professional and technical staff (Fig. 37). There has

36 National Health Service spending (£ millions)

	1972–3	1982–3
Hospitals & Community health	1535	9743
General Medical Services (mainly GPs)	212	972
Drugs	285	1605
Dental services	132	627
Opthalmic services	31	257
Payments by patients	90	417

been a smaller increase in the often criticised area of administration and ancillary staff.

Life expectancy has risen, so there are more old people. Many of these need medical care, some for medical problems, but increasing numbers for mental problems linked with growing old. Over 40% of the money spent on hospital and community

services goes on the care of old people. While efforts can be made to have old people looked after by their families, and by local volunteers, in many cases specialist care is needed, and this is expensive.

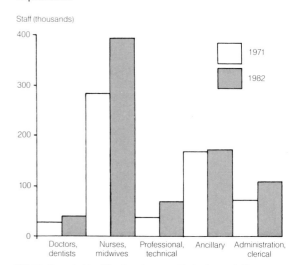

37 National Health Service staff (selected figures) in England (thousands)

The Conservative Government elected in 1979 thinks that savings can be made in some areas of the Health Service. For example, 10% of the NHS budget is 'hotel' charges, for laundry, cleaning and catering. Health Authorities have been encouraged to use private companies to do these jobs at a lower cost than the NHS 'in-house' staff. But trade unions have been against this as they claim standards have been lowered, and that the private companies often hire staff for shorter hours, at lower wage rates and under poorer working conditions. There have been suggestions that doctors could cut costs by ordering fewer tests, X rays and drugs, and by sending patients home earlier than they might do. They have also been asked to prescribe cheaper drugs in place of brand-name drugs (e.g. 'NOPain' instead of aspirin). In general, doctors insist that they keep their right to treat patients as they think best, and not by the cheapest method. It is possible, however, to cut costs for some hospital supplies by careful buying (things like paper towels, for example), without endangering patients or angering staff.

While these plans might save money, they cannot make much difference to the huge cost of the NHS. National Insurance contributions cover less then 10% of this, and prescription and other charges less than 3%. Putting these charges up would only bring in a little money. Other suggestions have included making patients pay 'hotel' charges while

hospital and decreasing staffing levels, but both
these have met with strong opposition.

PRIVATE MEDICINE

The Conservative Government elected in 1979
encourages private medicine. They want more
people to pay into private medical schemes such as
BUPA and believe that this will relieve pressure on
the NHS. All workers pay National Insurance contributions, but those who wish can also join a private
health insurance scheme for which they pay a
monthly premium. If they become ill, these people
can then choose a private bed in an NHS hospital,
or a private hospital or nursing home with specialist
treatment if they need it. The health insurance
company pays most of the costs. In 1982, more than
3 million people were covered by private health
insurance, many through group or workers'
schemes arranged by employers.

The arguments for and against private medicine

FOR
    Treatment is prompt and at a convenient time
    Enables people to choose which doctor or
    consultant to be treated by
    Provides 'luxury' accommodation in private
    rooms instead of wards
    Provides top-quality food
    Removes some patients from NHS waiting lists
    Health insurance schemes can be offered as
    fringe benefit in jobs
    High standard of medical care possible with
    plenty of staff
    Gives people the right to choose the treatment
    they think best by paying for it

AGAINST
    Takes only short-term patients so leaves chroni-
    cally sick and mentally ill to NHS
    Expense is on top of National Insurance contri-
    butions and taxes which pay for NHS
    Uses NHS trained staff, reducing the workforce
    available for NHS patients
    Uses NHS laboratories and equipment, so leng-
    thening NHS waiting lists
    Run as a 'business' rather than a caring service
    Makes people's health dependent on their
    wealth
    Tries to make NHS appear second rate
    Creates a two-tier health service with privileged
    treatment for those who can afford it

CURING THE ILLS OF THE NHS

Madge Bailey has spent a lot of time in hospital
during the last few years as she has a chronic
illness.

38 A protest about the opening of a private hospital

'Last time I was in, we had paper sheets – not very
comfortable. The laundry was on strike in protest
because the government wanted a private company to do the work.

This hospital is much better than it used to be. I
should know – I've been here often enough! New
wards were opened a few years ago, and a lot of
new equipment was brought in to help treat
people. They can do much more complicated
operations here now. People used to have to
travel miles to get to a bigger hospital years ago.

The staff are excellent. The nurses work very
hard yet they are cheerful and always there when
you need them. When I broke my arm, they
treated me very quickly in Casualty, even
although they were busy. But you can see the
hospital is short of money. Some of the wards are
a bit shabby – that doesn't matter much. But they
are also short of staff: one trained nurse between
two wards at night, with only students and
auxiliaries to make up the numbers – it doesn't
seem right! And that private hospital down the
road is just the opposite – lots of money to spend
on carpets and colour televisions. I suppose the
food might be nicer there, but they wouldn't have
fixed my broken arm since they don't do casualty.
In any case I wouldn't be accepted on a health
insurance scheme – I'm too old and I've been too
ill for too long.'

1. How is the NHS paid for?
2. Describe the major problems facing the NHS.
3. What efforts can be made to save money in the NHS? What changes might this make to the service provided?
4. Do you think private medicine should be encouraged? Give reasons for your answer.

Housing

The government supplies local authorities with money to provide council housing as part of the Welfare State. Although the number of people who own council houses or who buy their own home through a mortgage loan is increasing, large numbers of people rent accommodation, and most of these rent from the local authority.

HOUSING STOCK

In general, housing standards have improved over the last 30 years and, over the country as a whole, the number of houses is roughly equal to the number of households (although there are imbalances in some areas). However, as the following statistics for Scotland show, there are still many unsatisfactory houses, of which a large proportion are council houses.

In 1980 Scotland had 1 997 000 dwellings

of which
- 104 000 were structurally unsound or had rising damp
- 150 000 had damp and condensation problems
- 150 000 were overcrowded
- 150 000 were empty because of moves or repairs

Obviously some houses are counted in more than one category in the table: they might be overcrowded and damp for example. Extensive repair work is needed to bring some of these houses up to an acceptable standard, at a time when many local authorities are being told to cut back on spending. A further problem is that the size of house available for rent from local authorities does not always suit the size of the families who want to rent. While 52% of households are one or two people, only 14% of local authority houses have one or two apartments. At the other end of the scale, 13% of households have more than five people, but only 4% of local authority houses have more than five rooms. Also, the overall figures for housing hide the fact that in some areas of Britain there is a serious

40 (a) Tenure of houses, Great Britain

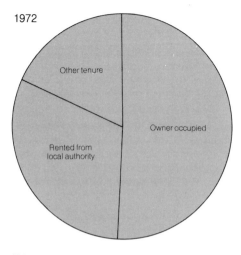

1972

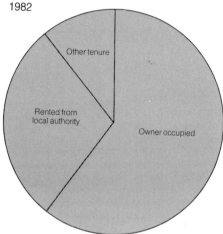

1982

(b) Housing stock, Great Britain

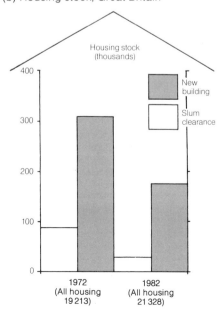

housing shortage (eg. growth areas and some rural areas) while other areas have a surplus of empty houses, particularly in post-war housing schemes and inner-city areas.

PUBLIC EXPENDITURE CUTS

The reduction in public expenditure which has been part of central government policy in the 1980s has affected local authority housing. There is less money available from central government for planned developments. The amount of money available for repairing and renovating older property has been cut too. In the early 1980s, the Conservative Government linked the amount of money that a local authority was able to borrow for modernisation and new building to its acceptance of government policy on rents and rates and council house sales. Many local authorities faced cuts in government loans because of this. The Conservative Government also 'fined' local authorities heavily if it was considered that they had overspent, so spending on housing has been badly hit.

THE HOUSING
(Homeless persons) ACT 1977

Under this Act, local authorities have to help the homeless. Normally a council decides who should get a council house by using a points system. The size of family, present living conditions, health and length of time on the waiting list are all important; single people and childless couples do not usually come high on the list as they cannot get many points. If a person has local connections (such as a job), has not made themselves intentionally homeless, and is in great need (with children to care for, old, handicapped or the victim of fire or flood) then the local council must provide that person with a council house. Many councils have been criticised for providing the poorest possible accommodation, however, or for refusing people whom they think do not have a good claim.

TENANTS' RIGHTS ACT 1980

The most important result of this Act was that it gave council tenants the right to buy their council house at a special price (much lower than it would cost if it was sold privately). The newspaper report of a council meeting and the case study which follow show that feelings run high on this issue.

Sale of the Century Claim

At last week's housing sub-committee meeting, Councillor Pettigrew hit out at the low prices being asked for council houses. He said 'Ratepayers and taxpayers have paid for these excellent houses. Now they are being sold off, sometimes at half the market price! No wonder so many tenants in Firpark are rushing to buy – it's the sale of the century!' Councillor Graham, his Labour colleague on the committee, agreed and began to speak but was interrupted by the Chairperson, Councillor Joan Meek. 'This is no place to go over old arguments. Our tenants now have the right to buy their homes; after all, they have been paying rent for many years to earn this special deal, and they have shown by their votes for the Conservative Party at local elections that many of them agree with this policy.'

At this point Councillor Birch showed the housing account for the past few years. He pointed out the large surplus last year as a result of money raised through selling the council houses, and pointed out the likely drop in repair bills with fewer houses in the council stock.

Councillor Graham then produced tables showing which council houses were sold. She commented, 'All the best houses in the good areas are being sold off. In a year or two we'll be left with the run-down houses in the most unpleasant areas, and a huge repair bill with less rent income. The idea that selling off council houses mixes communities is nonsense.' Councillor Pettigrew added that, with a growing waiting list, the council was foolish to follow central government rulings so enthusiastically. There were not enough council houses he said. Councillor Meek moved on to the next item on the agenda; the eviction of tenants in rent arrears.

OUR HOUSE

'When we accepted this house, we were absolutely desperate. We couldn't stay with my parents any longer, not with the baby.

The rent isn't too high, but the heating bills are dreadful. One of the bedrooms is damp and the council people who came to look at it say I should heat the room more. I just can't afford to. I think there's something wrong with the building, but they say I shouldn't dry nappies indoors.

Where should I dry them? They'd be stolen off the line on the drying green.

This area seems to be a dumping ground for bad tenants. Nothing but troublemakers and people like us who are desperate for a house, any house. Not much chance of getting anywhere else. It'll take us years to get enough points and a reputation as good tenants to get a nice council house with a garden: if any are left by then—most are being bought by the people living in them. Why can't they buy other houses and leave the decent council houses for people like us who'll never be able to afford to buy our own house?'

Questions

1. What are Britain's major housing problems in the 1980s?
2. What effect have the public expenditure cuts of the 1980s had on housing?
3. Give the arguments for and against the sale of council houses.

41 A protest about rent rises

Education

Education sets out to develop the abilities of children so that they can play a full part in modern society. Most education takes place in schools, colleges and universities. The 1980s are a time of great change in education. Many school rolls are falling as there are fewer children of secondary school age. Many school pupils of over 16 are staying on longer at school because there is high youth unemployment. New subjects such as computing and technology are being introduced and examined, while the more traditional subjects are being tested in new ways.

COMPULSORY EDUCATION

The government, and most people, think that children need a carefully planned education to fit them for life in the modern world. If this education was not compulsory some parents might be tempted to send children out to work, or keep them at home to help out in the house or with the family business, as happened many years ago. However, it is appreciated that some parents might feel very strongly about educating their own children and, they can satisfy the education authorities that they are providing a good eduction, they are not breaking the law.

COMPREHENSIVE OR SELECTIVE EDUCATION

A major issue which divides people, particularly along political party lines, is that of selection in education. Some people favour selecting the cleverest children and sending them to one type of school (often called 'grammar' schools) to study mainly academic subjects among other bright, interested pupils. The remaining less able children, most of whom will leave school at 16, would go to other schools (sometimes called 'secondary modern' schools) to follow more practical courses. Supporters of selective schools believe both the intelligent and less intelligent pupils receive a better, more appropriate, education if they are educated separately. Most pupils in Britain attend comprehensive schools introduced by the Labour Government from the 1960s. These schools take in all children from the surrounding area and offer a wide variety of courses. Supporters of comprehensive schools feel the social mix of pupils in these schools is important and that all children will have an equal opportunity to develop their full potential.

2 High technology education in a comprehensive school in the 1980s

INDEPENDENT OR STATE SCHOOL

A further educational issue which divides along party lines is whether there should be schools which are privately run, not State run. While State schools are run on government money, independent schools depend on income from fees, usually paid by parents of the pupils. The Conservative Party encourages the growth of independent schools and allows local authorities to pay fees for a number of pupils to attend. They also offer assisted places for pupils whose parents could not otherwise afford to send them to these schools. The Labour Party believes that such schools reinforce the divisions between rich and poor, and that often the more able and highly motivated pupils go to these schools, instead of making their contribution to the life of a State school.

Questions

1. Why is education compulsory?
2. Outline the different ways in which a school could become selective.
3. What are the views of the two major political parties on independent schools?

The Social Worker

The thinking behind the Welfare State is that a complex set of services and provisions have been established to care for those who are entitled to them. The effective operation of these services can often best be achieved through the work of the Social Work departments set up by local authorities.

'I suppose I see myself as a sort of link person between my clients and the agencies that can help them: Social Security departments, home helps, psychologists. I'm also a bit of a trouble-shooter: I'll try to sort things out if a marriage is in trouble, or if a teenager falls out with parents. If an old person isn't coping well, I try to help – not by washing up dishes – but chatting over a cup of tea. I act as a friend and point out what help is available from other people. If old people really can't manage on their own any longer I might suggest a day care unit, a move to sheltered housing, or, if they need a lot of help, a residential home.

I am able to put pressure on housing departments to get special housing for handicapped or ill people. I can show people how to budget better – to sort out which bills they have to pay now, to come to special arrangements with the electricity board to pay off debts, to get extra payments from the DHSS if possible.

Some of my work is with kids in trouble. Some are really bad ones, kids I know will spend a lot of their lives in prison. But lots are just a bit wild or unhappy. These are the ones who truant from school, or get into trouble with the police. I try to talk to them and help them sort out their lives better. Some end up living away from home in children's homes or Approved Schools. I work with them to help them prepare for life "outside". Others live with their parents, but I visit to keep an eye on them – supervision it's called. Since I work in Scotland, I write Court Reports for adult offenders, work with them when they are on probation or parole, and help them once they leave prison.

I spend a lot of time with foster parents, from helping select them in the first place, to giving support once a child is placed with a family. I do the same sort of work with families who are thinking of adopting children with "special needs": perhaps a handicapped child.

A few cases get priority. I have to drop everything if a case of a battered child comes up. It's my responsibility to see that the child is safe. Sometimes I feel as if the troubles of the world are on my caselist. And there are days when the reports I have to write seem endless. But I think I do a vital job. I make sure the Welfare State works for people who really need it.'

5. Law and Order

In a civilised society, people recognise the need for laws. Elected representatives draw up the laws on behalf of the people of the country. It is part of democracy that people agree to obey these laws, even if they don't like them.

The basis of many laws is the protection of the rights of the individual. Important ones include the right to life, freedom from torture, the right to privacy, peaceful enjoyment of property and the right to a fair trial. If anyone infringes another's rights on these or other basic rights, legal action can be taken against them. The laws make sure people and their property are safeguarded. Civil law deals with disputes between individuals, while in criminal law, the State acts to protect society, as a whole.

England and Wales, Scotland and Northern Ireland each have their own legal systems, so it is not always possible to examine trends in crime for the UK as a whole. It must also be remembered that the figures in 'crime' tables are not a very true indication since the size of the police workforce in some areas, and police priorities, may mean that many crimes are unreported or undetected. Crimes of violence are on the increase – they doubled in England and Wales between 1971 and 1980 but these crimes still make up less than 5% of all serious offences.

43 Serious offences recorded by police, England & Wales (per 100 000 people)

	1972	1981
Homicide	1	1
Violence against person (excl. homicide)	106	202
Sexual offences	48	39
Burglary	895	1465
Robbery	18	41
Theft & handling stolen goods	2059	3248
Fraud & forgery	221	216
Criminal damage	85	784

Detection and Enforcement

THE POLICE FORCE

Each British police force is responsible for enforcing law in its own area, but also works with other areas, and depends on ordinary people's co-operation. In Britain, as a whole, there is one police officer for every 500 people. Police work includes the protection of people and property, patrolling and traffic control, crime prevention, criminal investigation, the apprehension of offenders and community liaison. The main departments of the police force are the uniformed department, the Criminal Investigation Department (CID), the traffic department, and specialised departments, such as the mounted branch and dog handlers.

The law is also enforced by Customs and Excise officials, the Inland Revenue, Immigration Officers, Factory Inspectors, Traffic Wardens and the Office of Fair Trading.

All sorts of scientific aids and up-to-date technology are used to track down and detect criminals. Computers store police records and speed up the sorting and checking of information. In major enquiries, each statement and piece of information can be fed into a computer and then checked against already stored details for possible leads. This helps police track down and arrest criminals more quickly.

THE PUBLIC IMAGE

People who are the victims of crime might complain that there are not enough police and that they are ineffective. Those who are arrested for petty breaches of the law might complain of too many police. The balance has to be achieved between a 'police state' where police are powerful and control most aspects of people's lives, and 'anarchy' where there is no effective rule of law. Many police forces feel they get too little support from the general public. Strong feelings are aroused when police stop and search large numbers of people. Yet there is a general feeling, especially in the popular press, that we live in a violent society.

A public debate between two police chiefs in the early 1980s centred on two major types of policing. Community policing takes the police closer to the community by putting police back on 'the beat'. The police officer becomes a familiar local face, and gains the confidence of local people. It is claimed that many crimes are prevented because of local knowledge, and others are detected more quickly. 'Fire Brigade' or reactive policing involves a police force more remote from the local people. When an incident is reported the police move in quickly with a high-technology back up. Experts disagree on the balance between these two types of policing.

44 Police working with computers

Special Patrol Groups are specially trained police units. They have come to public notice in riot control and anti-terrorist activities. The work of the political Special Branch includes investigating terrorism and subversive activity. Although the police on normal duties do not carry guns, there has been a lot of public concern about the increasing number of occasions when firearms have been used, and in what circumstances police should be armed.

When a complaint is made against the police, the police themselves investigate. This practice has been widely criticised, especially in the light of complaints following the 1981 inner-city riots. The Scarman Report into these riots suggested many changes should be made in police recruitment, training and policing generally. More black police were recommended; a more independent complaints procedure; training in race relations and dealing with immigrant and black communities; and a return to police on 'the beat'.

Prosecution and Trial

In Scotland (unlike the rest of Britain) the police and other investigative agencies do not decide on charges of guilt or innocence: this is the task of the courts. Nor do they decide if a case will be pursued: the evidence is presented to the Procurators Fiscal and they decide whether to go ahead with the case through the courts. It is a basic point of law throughout Britain that any people who are accused of a crime are innocent until their guilt is proved beyond reasonable doubt.

When someone has been charged with a crime, the court procedure follows a pre-determined format. The accused will have his or her case tried in the court relevant to the alleged crime. This is fixed by Act of Parliament and normally depends on the age of the accused (in Scotland, those under sixteen must be reffered to a children's panel which is not officially a court of law) or on the seriousness of the alleged crime.

All accused have the right to a defence. If their financial position is below a certain level they are entitled to legal aid, i.e. a defence lawyer whose fee will be paid from the public purse.

In the court all activity must follow the legal and proper procedure. The prosecution present their case and witnesses. The defence have the right to question these witnesses. Then the defence have the opportunity to present their case and witnesses who may be cross-examined by the prosecution. After both sides have summed up, the decision will be made by the magistrate or sherriff. When it is a jury trial, the sheriff or judge will sum up and then await the jury's verdict. (In Scotland the jury has fifteen members, majority verdicts are accepted and they may find the person charged, 'guilty', or 'not guilty' or 'not proven'.) Afterwards anyone found guilty may appeal against conviction and/or sentence. Any such appeal will be heard by judges of the Court of Appeal.

The maximum sentence possible for any crime is stated within the relevant Act of Parliament, and the court may not exceed this. Possible sentences include fines, probation, suspended sentences, imprisonment or a period of community service.

PUNISHMENT

In considering a suitable sentence for a guilty person, the court is expected to take into account the reason for punishment. This may be one, or a combination, of the following: to discourage others from committing the same crime (this often means a severe punishment); to give a punishment that fits the crime; to protect society from the criminal; to discourage the criminal from repeating the crime; to compensate society or the aggrieved person.

Capital punishment, hanging, was abolished by Parliament in 1965. Since then MPs have several times voted with large majorities against bringing it back as the ultimate punishment.

MARY

It had been several years since Mary's mother felt she had any control over her nine-year-old daughter. The youngest of a family of four, Mary had had her own way all her life and saw no reason why she should do what her mother or her father or her teachers asked. She pleased herself: she seldom went to school, she stayed out late playing football with the boys and hanging about outside the Youth Club: she'd been thrown out of there so often that she had been banned for life.

The school and social worker finally decided that Mary was beyond the control of her parents and that they should refer her case to the Reporter of the Children's Panel.

A social worker called at the house and talked about Mary with her parents. Then, a report was sent to the Reporter. The school also sent some information about Mary's attendance, behaviour and performance at school.

Mary's parents got quite a shock when the offical documents inviting them to attend the hearing arrived, especially as they read the bits about penalties if they failed to attend the hearing. They decided to take Mary's uncle with them to help them. He was a youth leader in a local Church and they felt they could use his support.

The hearing itself surprised them – much less formal than they had imagined – just the three panel members (ordinary folk!), the Reporter, and the social worker they'd met before.

The hearing began with the chairman of the panel explaining the grounds for referral – that Mary was out of control of her parents – and asked if Mary understood what this meant. Mary's parents hoped Mary wouldn't be her usual cheeky self and were quite amazed when she answered politely. Mary's mother, after making a series of excuses, finally accepted that Mary was out of her control and that her husband didn't really have much to do with the child.

The panel members took quite a time discussing with Mary and her parents what was in each of the reports they had about her and her family. Mary's mother knew she hadn't really tried to make Mary behave. Often she was quite pleased when Mary stayed out late because at least she wasn't around the house all the time. She realised now that if she wanted to avoid Mary being sent away – perhaps to a children's home – she would have to show the panel that she would try her best to keep Mary under control. If she didn't manage better with Mary at home, under the supervision of the social worker, it would be reported at the next review hearing.

Questions

1. What basic rights are laws in Britain designed to protect?
2. What are the main duties of the police?
3. Why do the police arrest but not try; why does the jury try but not prosecute; why does a judge sentence but not try?
4. What part do each of the following play in the legal system? witness, police, jury, judge, lawyer, traffic warden, factory inspector.
5. In what ways and for what reasons would the following three people receive different sentences?

   Ann stole babyfood from a supermarket. She lives on State Benefits, and, after paying for new shoes for her child, had no money left for food for the baby.

   Jenny, as part of a gang, held up a post office at gunpoint and stole several thousand pounds.

   Frank was out with a friend shooting rabbits. There was an accident. Frank's gun went off and killed his friend.

6. Social Issues

Multi-cultural Britain

British society contains many people who have come, or whose ancestors have come, from different cultures and countries. Although these people have made their home in Britain, they have kept many of the tastes and ways of life of their original countries. The rich variety of foods, customs, words, clothes, music and religions which are part of British culture today can be traced back to these **immigrant** groups.

However, not everyone in Britain appreciates the richness of a multi-cultural society. Some people resent immigrants coming to Britain and changing traditional ways of life. They may regard people from other cultures as inferior because of their colour or 'different' behaviour, and this leads to **discrimination** against non-white people in jobs, education and daily life.

In the 1950s large numbers of coloured immigrants from Commonwealth countries were encouraged to come to Britain to fill jobs in the postwar boom. By the early 1960s, however, many people believed that immigration had become too high and should be restricted. They felt that Britain was storing up trouble for itself in the future by allowing so many immigrants into the country, and that cultural differences would lead to serious conflict. These feelings were expressed forcefully by one MP, Enoch Powell, in 1968 when he said: 'As I look ahead I am filled with foreboding. Like the Roman, I seem to see the River Tiber foaming with much blood.'

The response of different governments to this supposed threat has taken two main lines. One has been to limit the number of coloured immigrants; the other has been to try to establish better relations between white and black people in Britain.

Since 1962, governments have introduced a series of laws designed to restrict immigration into Britain, particularly of coloured people from the 'New Commonwealth'. Previously almost all members of the Commonwealth had the right to come and settle in the mother country. By the Nationality Act of 1981, this right was limited to people whose parents or grandparents were born in the UK.

As Table 45 shows, the number of black residents in the UK is a tiny fraction of the total population. Even in areas with the largest concentration of blacks, the proportion is still quite small. The Immigration Acts have limited immigration, but, because they apply particularly to people from the New Commonwealth, they have discriminated against non-white immigrants. In 1983, fewer people emigrated from Britain than came to live here, but this was the first time this had happened in almost 20 years. Moreover, of the 200 000 immigrants, over half were from the European Community and the USA.

The second government intervention has been in the area of race relations. Laws have been introduced which protect people entitled to live here from unfair discrimination 'on the grounds of colour, race or ethnic or national origin'. By Race Relations Acts of 1965, 1968 and 1976, this discrimination was made illegal in the provision of goods and services, employment and training, education, housing and advertising. The Commission for Racial Equality (CRE) works towards getting rid of unfair treatment and tries to encourage equality of opportunity regardless of the colour of a person's skin.

But passing laws does not change the attitudes of all prejudiced people. A study by the CRE, published in 1980, showed that there was still discrimination against young black people applying for jobs. The CRE arranged for a mixed group of young people to send letters in answer to a large number of job adverts in local newspapers. Results showed that one application from a white person

45 UK selected population statistics (1981 census)

	UK	Greater London	West Midlands	Scotland
Total population	53 556 911	6 608 598	2 628 419	5 035 315
UK birth	50 197 086	5 405 576	2 370 422	4 894 372
Old Commonwealth *	152 747	37 064	3 308	15 292
New Commonwealth †	1 325 175	595 243	130 332	33 223
Other	1 274 475	371 255	63 852	65 384

* Mainly white from e.g. Canada, Australia, New Zealand.   † Mainly black from e.g. India, West Indies.

was far more likely to succeed than one from an equally well qualified and experienced black person. There are many other instances of similar discrimination, yet it is very difficult to prove that an individual has been discriminated against simply on the grounds of race or colour.

Changes in people's attitudes come very slowly. Sometimes it is a matter of making people more aware of the need to adapt to a multi-cultural society. For example, schools which at one time insisted on school uniforms are now more prepared to allow variation in uniform to fit in with cultural and religious traditions. Similarly, school meals are now more varied.

Governments have found race relations a particularly difficult area in which to use legislation to enforce change. Some of the laws have been 'panic' measures to deal with sudden and unexpected surges of immigration (e.g. as a result of the expulsion of Asians with British passports from East African countries). Other measures, such as putting money into inner-city areas where many blacks live, have been in response to the riots of 1981. In the summer of that year, violence broke out in several cities in England, and in some cases the riots were initially caused by friction between blacks and whites. The Scarman Report which investigated the riots blamed them on poor relations between largely black communities and largely white police forces, and on policing methods generally. Clearly much goodwill by all involved in community relations is required in order for Britain to obtain the full benefits of the mixture of citizens entitled to live here.

Questions

1. Why might Britain be described as being a multi-cultural society?
2. What was Enoch Powell predicting in 1968?
3. What attempts have governments made to limit immigration?
4. What does the 1981 census show about the proportion of black people in the UK?
5. What efforts have been made to reduce discrimination against non-whites? Why have these not been entirely successful?
6. Suggest some possible uses of money in the inner-city areas to improve race relations.

Leisure

People in Britain have much more leisure time in the 1980s than they had in the past. The average working week for manual workers has fallen (from 46 hours in 1970 to 44 hours in 1981). Annual holidays have increased from two weeks (taken in summer) to four to six weeks (often taken as summer and winter holidays) plus a number of extra days throughout the year. There is the enforced leisure time of the 3.5 million unemployed, and also, in general, people have more free time because of labour-saving devices in the home, such as automatic washing machines. This means that there is a vast leisure market to be exploited. And this market is likely to continue to grow as people retire earlier, technology replaces workers, and the length of the working week falls further.

There has never before been such a wide range of leisure pursuits on offer. Traditional cinema going, dancing, football playing and spectating have been supplemented by newer activites such as keep-fit classes, jogging, do-it-yourself projects and computer games. This wide range of activities has forced some previously well-established leisure industries to face up to the challenge of competition.

Alternative attractions to the traditional Saturday afternoon activity of going to a football match meant that some football clubs faced commercial ruin as attendances fell and expenses rose. Many supporters chose to do other things and watch football on television in the evening. Star footballers demanded higher wages for attracting crowds. Many clubs have met the challenge by modernising their grounds to make them safer and more comfortable, including all-seated stadiums. Sponsorship has brought in more money. Some clubs are even adapting their grounds for other activities so that they can bring in money from ventures other than football, all year round. Football is a business and cannot keep running at a loss.

Many of the new forms of leisure activity are based on high technology. Video machines allow television viewers to see more programmes and rent films, and potential audiences are enormous: 2 million more people had television sets in 1982 than in 1972; 30% of British homes owned a video in 1983, compared with 4% in 1980. Television games and computers are among the most popular leisure facilities in the home.

In the past, spare time was mainly a rest from work and was used for relaxation and enjoyment. Now, however, it is often more than simply time to 'recharge the batteries' ready for more work. Work is no longer a very important part of everyone's life. Many people are unemployed and many others are in monotonous or unfulfilling jobs. More and more people therefore want to find stimulation and challenges in their leisure activities.

Increasing numbers of people make use of

46 A marathon run

leisure for educational purposes by enroling in the Open University, evening classes, or community education. This can be to obtain specific qualifications, or simply learning for interest. The number of different magazines available (from 4460 in 1972 to over 6000 in 1983) also reflects the wide variety of interests, and the increase in reading generally. Book publishers now offer their most popular titles in supermarkets, and launch new titles with magazine and television advertising.

Health has become a major leisure industry. During the 1970s, interest in health foods and more nutritious cookery was accompanied by an increased desire to get fit and keep fit. Jogging, fun runs and marathons, once minority interests, are now popular events. Aerobics, jazz-dance and exercise-to-music classes enjoy a mass following. A large 'spin-off' industry of specialised clothing, workout books and records has built up round this leisure craze.

It is acceptable for people to save money or even make money during leisure time. Do-it-yourself is a major industry, and creativity can be financially rewarding by the sale of products such as hand-made toys, paintings, knitted goods. Betting on horses and dogs, and a night (and afternoon) at bingo continue to be popular, while new casinos open up a whole new area for the gambler: 39% of the public gamble in some form regularly.

While the right to leisure and the freedom to use it is widely accepted, there are some areas of concern. When people are faced with a large amount of leisure time, because they are unemployed for example, it is very easy for this to result in boredom and idleness. Apathy and depression can lead people to fill their idle time with anti-social behaviour such as crime or excessive drinking or drug taking. There is also a great temptation for people to fill their leisure time lazily: by watching television and videos instead of actively taking part in something. Has the provision of 'armchair' entertainment turned Britain into a nation of spectators rather than participators? If this is so, then the increase in sports centres, community education centres, youth clubs and activity holidays, can ensure that at least the opportunity is there. The individual can then decide what to do with this rapidly changing lifestyle: to watch or take part.

Questions

1. Why do people have more leisure time than they used to?
2. In what ways have each of the following faced up to the challenge of competition?: football clubs; dance halls; cinemas; television.
3. What opportunities are there for (a) education; (b) fitness; (c) making or saving money during leisure time?
4. Describe the ways in which people in Britain have opportunities to (a) spectate and (b) participate during their leisure time.

A Woman's Place

By the 1960s and 1970s, the model of a woman as a housewife staying at home to look after the children was a very outdated one. Most women went out to work. Labour-saving kitchen and cleaning equipment meant that housework was less time-consuming. Families expected to have the higher living standards which came with having two parents at work. More reliable family planning methods allowed women to decide when to have children, and so plan to continue their career. As divorce laws changed, there were more one-parent families, often headed by women. (Only 3% of families consist of mother, father and two children, although this is the 'standard' presented by the **media**.) But many working women found they were paid less than men for the same work. They felt they were often passed over for jobs simply because they were women. Borrowing money and getting promotion could also be more difficult for them.

Trade unions, women's groups and the Women's Liberation Movement campaigned for more equal treatment for women: in particular, equal pay and an end to sex discrimination. The Equal Pay Act and the Sex Discrimination Act came into operation in the late 1970s, and the Equal Opportunities Commission was set up to provide back-up, information and to fight cases. Yet in some ways women are no more equal now than they were before.

As Fig. 47 shows, women's pay position has not improved significantly. This is partly because many women still tend to work in traditionally 'female' occupations such as nursing, which are also traditionally low paid. Also some jobs, such as shop work, are not highly unionised, so workers get little help to fight for equal pay. Many women work part-time, or work from home where some of the laws do not apply.

The media continues to present the image of 'wife and mother' at home, while the reality is very different. Most wives and mothers now go out to work, and an increasing number of women now choose to remain single or not to have children. Yet even these women are very unlikely to 'make it to the top'. It is still men who dominate in the fields of politics, television, advertising and journalism, particularly in managerial positions. People are slow to change their attitudes. Many men still regard women as inferior in business, and women have to fight to be taken seriously and treated fairly. Working mothers face the added difficulties of having to arrange for someone to look after the children, and coping with running a family home. Those who are well paid can afford to hire nannies and house-keepers; others have to rely on State-run nurseries, child minders, and unlimited supplies of energy. Women with children are often turned down for promotion because there is still a tendency to consider them 'unreliable' in responsible jobs.

Government cuts affect women particularly badly. Nurseries have closed, and many of the traditional female jobs have gone. With increased unemployment, the view is sometimes expressed that working women should give up their jobs to men, the traditional wage earners. Cuts in welfare services mean that more old and handicapped people are to be cared for in the community, at home with some assistance from local care centres. The Conservative Government elected in 1979 has re-emphasised the position of the family as a vital part of the community. This means that the load of caring for those who cannot manage by themselves generally falls on women. So, while women are still trying to establish themselves as equal members of society, there is some pressure for them to resume a more old fashioned role.

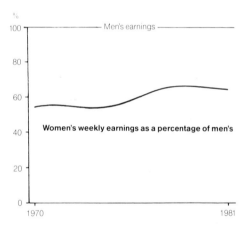

Women's weekly earnings as a percentage of men's

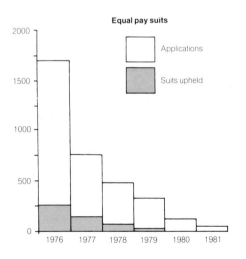

Questions

1. How has the role of women changed since the 1950s?
2. What discrimination do women sometimes face when they try for jobs?
3. Why is equality for women resisted by many groups of people? Mention: some men's attitudes; government; some employers; some women's attitudes; the media.

47 Some statistics on women at work